THE Catholic Guide TO Dating AFTER Divorce

"As a canon lawyer, I found that this book contains the clearest and most understandable explanation I've ever heard about the reasons the Church provides the annulment process, and why saving sexual intimacy for marriage is the best way to show respect for oneself, for one's partner, and for God. Highly recommended."

Sandra Makowski, S.S.M.N.
Chancellor
Diocese of Charleston, South Carolina

"As a Catholic who has been divorced, annulled, and remarried, I can say from personal experience that this book is desperately needed. So many divorced Catholic men and women still feel called to the vocation of marriage and want to pursue that calling within the context of the faith they hold so dear. Thank you, Lisa Duffy, for giving divorced Catholics a guidebook to help them find their way to the future they desire and deserve."

Mary DeTurris Poust
Author of *Cravings*

"The Holy Spirit has truly blessed Lisa with gifted insight into unlocking the joy of healing, forgiveness, and reconciliation after divorce. Jesus, the Supreme Healer, has always invited those who struggle to come close to his Sacred Heart, so that they can receive his Divine Mercy. Lisa Duffy, in her book *The Catholic Guide to Dating After Divorce,* leads the reader to this fount of hope, to experience in the healing waters of Christ's love the awe of a fresh start!"

Tom Peterson
Author, producer, and host of *Catholics Come Home*

"Lisa's guidebook to dating after divorce is a timely resource for Catholics free to marry again. I appreciated most the approach to helping annulled Catholics overcome their fears of dating again. I have worked with hundreds of divorced and annulled Catholics over the years, and this fear is very common (and understandable). If you feel this way, this book can help."

Anthony Buono
Founder
AveMariaSingles.com

"*The Catholic Guide to Dating After Divorce* is loaded with lots of good, practical ideas for the divorced person. My favorite part? That Lisa shares her own poignant, honest, and funny stories with a transparent and magnanimous heart!"

Rose Sweet
Author of *The Catholic's Divorce Survival Guide*

"Navigating the waters of life after divorce can be filled with deep emotions and confusion. Many of your friends may be nudging you along to find someone new, but are you ready to enter the dating scene again? If you have questions about dating after divorce, then keep Lisa Duffy's new book with you every step of the way. Lisa can help you on this journey because she has gone through it herself. Her gentle tone and truly compassionate nature are exactly what divorced Catholics need to overcome their fears, heal from past relationships, and reenter the dating scene with confidence."

Robyn Lee
Managing Editor
CatholicMatch Institute

"By taking the time to heal after a divorce, you can present the best version of yourself to the world and your suitor. Don't open yourself to dating before you open this book; it's that important!"

Heather Voccola
Columnist
CatholicMatch.com

Cultivating the 5 Qualities That Free You to Love

THE Catholic Guide TO Dating AFTER Divorce

Lisa Duffy

Ave Maria Press AVE Notre Dame, Indiana

Imprimatur and *Nihil Obstat*: Most Rev. Robert E. Guglielmone
Bishop of Charleston, South Carolina
August 21, 2014

Founded in 1865, Ave Maria Press is a ministry of the United States Province of Holy Cross.

www.avemariapress.com

Paperback: ISBN-13 978-1-59471-597-6

E-book: ISBN-13 978-1-59471-598-3

Cover image © Thinkstock.com.

Cover and text design by Katherine Robinson.

Printed and bound in the United States of America.

Library of Congress Cataloging-in-Publication Data is available.

To James Duffy, my incredible husband.
Thank you for all your love, inspiration, and support.
And, to my parents, Bernie and Gretchen Madrid.
Thank you for giving me the gift of life and my Catholic faith.

With special thanks to
Dan Flaherty, Lisa Hendey, Fr. Thomas Loya, Lisa Madrid,
Fr. Jonathan Morris, Brian Patrick, Tom Peterson, Amanda Rose,
Heidi Hess Saxton, and Rose Sweet.
I am grateful to each of you for your contribution to this book,
and appreciative of your time, your assistance,
your gracious encouragement, and your friendship.

Contents

Foreword

This is not just a book for divorced Catholics, despite what the title says. This is a book of hope for people like you and me, followers of Jesus, whose lives are messy because we are humans, and because we know other people whose lives are messy, and because their messy lives have affected ours.

Lisa Duffy has done what Pope Francis has been asking all of us to do. She has let down her guard and spoken boldly from her weakness in order to encourage you to do the same: to tell the Church your fears, your anxieties, your worries; tell her also your hopes, dreams, and aspirations.

And Lisa has done more than let down her guards and speak her heart. She's arisen from the ubiquitous state of newly single loneliness and desperation to be for you and me a sign of hopeful, joyful, post-trauma living. In this book she gives us a road map to live by as we pursue new beginnings.

As a priest, I've got a theory I try to live by. Actually, it's more than a theory. I believe it is as true as any proven scientific law. It comes from the Gospel where Jesus promises he is "the Way, the Truth, and the Life" (Jn 14:6). In practice, this life principle goes like this: No matter the situation in which we find ourselves, if we believe in Jesus and in his Church, and seek his face every day, there is always a very, very good solution to whatever predicament we find ourselves in, even the ones we have created for ourselves.

Are you divorced? Are you in an impossible relationship? Do you love your Church and yet feel so far away because of your sin or the sin of others? Welcome aboard! Our Church is made up of a motley crew, but as Francis has said, it's also a field hospital for us sinners.

So what is the solution when we have come out of a bad relationship and want to begin again, but don't know how? I've never been married, but because I have heard your confessions and wiped your tears, and because I have confessed my own sins, I know how far away even a repentant heart can feel from the love and mercy of God.

Here's the answer: No matter how far we feel from him, he is not far from us. And he is waiting to lead us into a new chapter of our lives, a chapter filled with unexpected and unimaginable blessings.

If you have begun or gone through the annulment process, then you are already moving in the right direction. You have already made an act of faith in Jesus and in his Church. You believe in Jesus' teaching on the indissolubility of marriage and you trust in the Church's authority to judge on matters of faith, morals, and the sacraments. You have already said, "Jesus, as much as this hurts, I'm sticking around because I'm pretty sure I'm still in love with you and your Church."

Do you think Jesus would remain distant from someone who has the nobility and courage to say that, and to live it out by faith each day? I don't. No way. Jesus is closest to those who suffer. And to those who suffer without losing faith, to them—and to you—he is most able to show his face, even if you have not seen him for many years.

In *The Catholic Guide to Dating After Divorce*, you will find balm for your wounds. You will find hope for your future. You will find practical steps for finding the person God has always had in store for you.

That's all. And that's a pretty good start.

Thank you, Lisa. I love both you and your husband, James, for who you are and what you have done for those who have suffered and for those who long to love like you do now, and to experience the wholeness that can only come by first acknowledging our brokenness.

Father Jonathan Morris
The New York Times bestselling author of
The Way of Serenity and *God Wants You Happy*

Introduction

What does your heart desire?

Since you have picked up this book, it's likely you want to find someone to fall in love with, someone who makes you happy and wants to be with you always. Maybe you are not convinced that getting into a new relationship is the right thing to do, but your friends and family are egging you on to get out there and find someone new. In addition to the uncertainty you might feel, this kind of pressure can make dating a stressful venture, too.

My friend, I know how you feel. After my divorce many years ago, I had many of the same desires and concerns. Although my first marriage was over, I believed wholeheartedly I still had a lot of love to give someone. I believed that, eventually, I could be a good wife and give a new marriage relationship every ounce of love and energy I had inside. I prayed hard to find the right person, and I started going out on dates. It didn't take me long to recognize that getting back into the dating scene and finding a new relationship was not as easy as my desire for finding love again made it seem.

But through much trial and error, I did find love again, and in the process of dating, grew to understand myself and my life goals much more than I ever had before. After taking the time to address festering emotional issues, learning how to rediscover myself and to remove the obstacles preventing me from finding happiness in a new relationship, I began dating again. Doing this due diligence opened up a totally new dimension to the whole dating process for me, helping me to discern God's will for my life. This was a critical step in getting to where I am today. Once I was able to accomplish these things, the rest was waiting to meet someone special. In time, I met an incredible man who became my best friend, and we have been happily married for almost fifteen years.

Five Attraction Factors

I would like to help you achieve whatever happiness awaits you, too, through the process of self-discovery that involves identifying the great things about yourself—things I like to call *attraction factors*. These five factors will help you become the best, most attractive version of yourself, and pave the way for you to experience greater satisfaction in your relationships, and to improve your ability to give and receive love.

Before we take a closer look at these attraction factors, let's address some of the initial, basic questions you might have about dating and relationships. You may have important questions, such as:

- *Everyone tells me it's time to get back out there and date . . . how do I know when I'm ready?*
- *I don't feel very attractive or loveable anymore. How can I change this?*
- *How can I make better choices in dating this time around?*
- *Should I be sexually involved with the person I am dating?*

These questions deserve answers, and I believe you will find them in this book. I wrote *The Catholic Guide to Dating After Divorce* specifically for you. I want to help you find the happiness you are looking for, but I also would like to save you a lot of heartache and wasted time.

Consider me a caddy of sorts, a companion to walk with you, support you, and offer advice as you play the dating game. It will be fun and sometimes funny, but there will also be some hard work to do. My goal is to help you become the most attractive version of yourself possible and with that, open a new chapter to your life, whether it is in finding an exciting, happy, and lasting relationship, or discovering some new path God has waiting for you. Are you ready?

Chapter One

Getting Ready to Love: Discovering the Best Version of Yourself

> For surely I know the plans I have for you, says the Lord, plans for your welfare and not for harm, to give you a future with hope.
>
> —Jeremiah 29:11

A great adventure awaits you, and I say that with confidence because I've walked in your shoes. I know what it is like to go through the process of rebuilding your life after divorce, wondering what the future holds. I know what it is like to sift through the debris of your former life and discover the truths, learn the hard lessons, and look to the future with resolve to make it better than the past. But make no mistake . . . despite all that, you are still positioned in a special and unique place in life.

In this new chapter, your life is like a block of clay, ready to be fashioned into something amazing, simply by seizing the opportunity. This time of being single is a gift from God to you. It may not feel like it is a gift at times. Rebuilding after divorce is hard work and it requires patience and persistence. But nevertheless, it is a wonderful opportunity to refine yourself emotionally and spiritually in a way that many people miss out on.

You might think of it this way: If you break a bone, the healing process that takes place actually makes your bone stronger than it was before. Homebuilders often use wood planks for framing that have been cut up into small pieces and adhered back together to make one long plank because that process makes the plank stronger. The same holds true for healing from a traumatic life event such as a divorce. The break is painful beyond words, but the healing process strengthens you in a way you had not been before. This will be an amazing time in your life if you open yourself to it and embrace the opportunities for change as they present themselves. In doing so, you will experience the joy of finding your new role in life and happiness in God's plan. How would I know? Allow me to share my story with you.

Hello, My Name Is "Divorced"

"What is your marital status?"

I stared at the impatient woman sitting behind her desk. *Marital status? Really?* I was opening a checking account, for Pete's sake. Why did she need to know that? Why did the bank need to know? Would they refuse my money if they didn't like my answer?

I was sensible enough to recognize I was over-reacting to a standard application inquiry but, frankly, at that moment the question felt like an open assault on my broken heart. I felt extremely defensive as my breath dissipated and my throat tightened. To Valerie, the young banking associate assisting me with this transaction, it was a simple question that required a simple answer. But to me, it was complicated.

Technically, the State of California had officially ruled my marriage was indeed null and void, and my ex-husband had sealed that deal by marrying someone else. Yet in my heart and according to the Catholic Church, I was still very married.

I was reluctant to answer this woman's question for another reason as well: I knew that, when I did, I would suddenly become less of a person in Valerie's eyes. Not married. *Divorced.*

She would never know that I had fought valiantly to save my marriage. No, she would never know how I begged my husband not to go, or how I swallowed my pride weeks later and asked him to consider reconciliation. She would never know how I prayed incessantly for God to bring him back and restore our marriage. She would never know these things because it wasn't part of her job to know or care, and it was inappropriate for me to tell her about them. Those details were not important; only my marital status was required.

"Divorced."

There, I said it. And I nearly choked on the horrible, nasty word. Valerie continued typing on the keypad, maintaining her poker face, and continuing on with her questions. A few minutes later we shook hands and I left, a new account owner. But I felt I had been stripped naked.

Obviously, I was having difficulty accepting my new social status. I didn't want to accept it because, no matter how bad things had become with my spouse, I married him with the expectation and the hope that we would be together forever. But now, my life had taken this unexpected turn and I had to start finding my true north again.

So now, I was being forced to affirm my new position in society through normal, everyday events such as filling out forms that required me to declare my social status or meeting new people and having to identify myself as "divorced." Attending family functions or Sunday Mass along with other happy families was a painful reminder of my failure. Even browsing the parish bulletin and reading about all the family activities being offered had its own special sting. To compound the fracture, by the time my husband had filed for divorce, I had suffered three miscarriages. These circumstances left me feeling somewhat cursed because at the age of thirty, I was divorced, childless, and without the hope of having children due to a surgery that, according to the doctors, had rendered me sterile. I felt completely alienated from the one thing in life I valued most . . . a happy family.

I share this story with you because I want you to know I understand where you are coming from. My guess is you can definitely relate to my story about having to publicly declare my divorce to others and no doubt have your own stories to tell. I was no different than many others who go through a divorce and wind up forgetting they are precious in God's sight. It is so easy to lose sight of the fact that we are loveable, valuable, and God still has great plans for us.

There is more life—exciting and happy life—waiting for you. Things have changed dramatically in my life for the better since that time in 1993, but it didn't happen quickly by any stretch of the imagination. It was a gradual, eye-opening process. At that time, I couldn't have imagined the kind of future I have now, but God is the most faithful Companion and the most loving of Healers, and it was through his grace and guidance I realized happiness was to be found in his plan, not in clinging to things that were dead and gone, things that were truly holding me back.

You are probably wondering what all this has to do with dating. Maybe you're not thinking about marriage yet, and are just wondering how to know when it's the right time to stick a toe in the shallow end of the dating pool. You want that happy and exciting life, and maybe even to get married again one day (or not)—but right now you just want to go out and have a little fun.

Fair enough. The fact that you are picking up a book about dating tells me that you want to go about this the right way, so that no one (including yourself) gets hurt. You've had enough heartache for one lifetime, and you are just starting to rebuild your sense of confidence and self-esteem. You want to know about those five qualities that free you to love—those "attraction factors."

But before we start looking at those five factors, we need to start by acknowledging where we are right now. I want you to feel assured the entire purpose of the discussions in this book are to help you move away from the negativity as you rebuild your life, start looking forward, and rediscover the incredibly attractive things about yourself that may have gotten lost as you went through your divorce.

Let's Talk about Dating

Dating is a process to help you recognize your new calling after a divorce. For many, dating will lead to a new relationship and ultimately to marriage. But, does this mean you should begin dating again as soon as the ink has dried on your divorce decree? Is it that assumed and automatic?

Re-entering the dating scene after going through a divorce can be an exciting but tricky process. The thought that someone might consider you attractive and worthwhile after enduring the soul-crushing ordeal of divorce may tempt you to short-circuit the healing that needs to take place before you are ready—emotionally, spiritually, or in any other way—for a dating relationship.

Dating as an adult after years of marriage and family life is a different experience from dating as a never-married adult. I have no doubt your goal in dating is to meet new people, enjoy new experiences, and move forward in rebuilding your life. These are all excellent goals and I would like to help you achieve them. But first let's take some time to talk this through before you make a move or accept an invitation to go out.

A Time to Build Up

> Therefore if anyone is in Christ, he is a new creature; the old things passed away; behold, new things have come.
>
> —2 Corinthians 5:17, NASB

The first time I reflected on this simple scripture passage I was on a silent retreat. As I read those words, it was if scales fell from my eyes and I finally recognized what had to be done. I had to let go of the past, forgive the hurts, and start moving forward. But the real epiphany came when I discovered I didn't have to do it all myself. I could start fresh, become a new creature in Christ if I let go of the old things and allow God to work things according to his plan. Those beautiful words from St. Paul became my life preserver and my inspiration in forging a new path. Over the course of many years, I became a completely new woman.

After going through the annulment process and experiencing an incredible level of healing along with receiving a decree of nullity, I moved forward and began dating. For a long period of time, I never found the right one. I then spent a brief period discerning a vocation to religious life, and soon after, I met the man to whom I am married today. We have been married nearly fifteen years and have three beautiful children despite the fact the doctors told me I would not be able to conceive a child. Yes, God truly does have his plans for our welfare!

You may already feel hopeful about finding a solid relationship that leads to a second marriage, and that is wonderful. But, maybe you are not quite to that point and this is fine, too. Either way, rest assured now is a great time to consider the ideas in this book. If you take them to heart, they can help you become a better person; someone who stands out and is noticed because of *who* you are, not simply because you might be physically appealing.

Whether or not you choose to enter into a new relationship, you want to feel as healed from your divorce as possible, no doubt, and as confident in yourself as you can. My goal is to help you rediscover yourself in ways that will elevate your level of attractiveness and give you confidence in your future. I hope the elements of my story I share with you will add to that sense of hope, regardless of the direction your life will take. I hope it will encourage you to trust God to lead you on the path to a happy life, no matter what has happened to you up to this point.

Letting Go of "Divorced"

Years ago on a Saturday morning, I spotted something that drove this point home for me. I was walking out the front door of St. Mary's Catholic Church where I had stopped to make a little visit before I headed off on my busy day, and driving past the church was a massive, muscled dude on a Harley Davidson motorcycle. And, he definitely fit the part: long hair, goatee, lots of leather, and tattoos. But what really caught my attention as he motored loudly past St. Mary's was that he made the Sign of the Cross. He was acknowledging Christ's real presence in the Eucharist contained within the tabernacle of the church, something my own parents had taught my siblings and me to do while we were growing up. He didn't seem to care in the least what an observer might think.

I was tickled at being able to witness that moment as I left the church. Who in the world would have thought some big, burly biker dude would be reverencing the Eucharist in public as he roared down Main Street?

No one would have expected that from a guy like him. And that is my point. People are far too quick to make blanket judgments:

"He's a biker, so he can't be a good Catholic." Or, "She's a single mother, so she can't be a good Catholic." Or, "They are divorced, so they can't be good Catholics."

Of course, none of these things are necessarily true, but the weight of these unjust judgments can cause great anguish that is even harder to bear when you are already feeling fragile and unlovable.

Ignoring the judgments of others who do not know your circumstances can be one of the most difficult aspects of rebuilding after divorce, but certainly one of the most important ones. That shameful, pernicious label of divorce can make you feel as if a rather conspicuous scarlet "D" is emblazoned on your chest and even people you meet in passing can tell just by looking at you that you are divorced. Any divorced person, especially a Catholic, will likely tell you this is one of the most painful aspects of losing a marriage and is most commonly experienced by the spouses who did not want the divorce to begin with. Despite their desire to make the marriage work, they are presumed to be "bad Catholics" by others because of the divorce.

It is true; people tend to judge what they do not know, which is not only uncharitable; but it is a slippery slope. But because we are not perfect human beings, we are all prone to making judgments at one point or another. The key to overcoming these judgments is to focus yourself on how God sees you.

> Love is the only mirror we must use to judge ourselves and others.
>
> —Bodie Thoene

An interesting twist in this dilemma is that many of us do not always receive these burdens from others; we often place our own judgments on ourselves. Why would someone who has been through the agony of divorce do this? Well, we know marriage is designed to be a permanent, life-long, exclusive relationship; when it falls apart, "failure" becomes the distinctive mark with which we brand ourselves practically by default. For this reason, primarily, it is easy to *assume* others are judging us because we are divorced.

Why Not Start Over at Another Church?

Any Catholic who has gone through a divorce is certainly aware of the Catholic Church's condemnation of divorce, which is based on the teachings of Christ regarding divorce and remarriage in Matthew 19:3–9. Most Catholics are raised to regard marriage as it was meant to be from the beginning: a permanent, exclusive, life-long union. So, it is understandable that someone might become so fearful of the judgment and reproach of other Catholics that he or she would give in to the temptation to avoid the source of the scrutiny altogether, to shy away from parish functions, attending Mass, and receiving the sacraments—the very source of healing and grace they need most.

Sadly, far too many divorced Catholics are living under the false assumption that Catholics who are divorced—even those who live an exemplary life—are not welcome at Mass and cannot receive the sacraments once they are issued a civil divorce decree. The truth is a civil divorce decree in and of itself does not prohibit one from receiving the sacraments. What does prohibit them from receiving is getting remarried without going through the annulment process and receiving a decree of nullity. But this misunderstanding and the harsh judgments that come with it cause them to leave the Church altogether. This is a crisis for two reasons. First, it is a crisis because generations of faith are lost when divorced parents leave the fullness of the faith and become members of Protestant churches, taking their children with them. But more than that, divorced Catholics who leave the Church are walking away from the very thing they need to heal: the sacraments. All the graces they need to get through their trials, rebuild their lives, and find happiness again are contained in the sacraments.

No matter what reactions you may have encountered from other people or what you think the Church teaches about divorce, you must remember you still are a significant and important member of the Body of Christ, and the place you will find the most healing is in your home, the Catholic Church.

You Are Not Alone

The first step in overcoming the burden of the label "divorced" is realizing you are not the only one it has happened to. There are many Catholics who have suffered the agony of divorce yet have gone on to live very happy lives. In my video documentary, *Voices of Hope*, more than twenty-five men and women from all walks of life and varying lengths of time being married spoke candidly about their experiences with the challenges of being a divorced Catholic. Here are a few of the things they shared about the assumptions they made and judgments they received:

> At first when I was going through my divorce I thought I couldn't go back to church. So not only was this the worst part of my life, but the thing I needed the most was not available to me. That was *really* hard.
>
> —Gianna

> There was a sense of shame and I felt like a failure. I didn't want to share what was going on with me with anyone. I didn't even tell my family what happened until about three months after it happened. I felt very alone. I felt discarded.
>
> —Kara

> It was particularly hard for me to continue going to Mass after my divorce. The people there knew me as a family man and judged me even though none of them knew my circumstances. A lot of our friends began avoiding me and the neighbor across the street forbade her son from playing with my son, which was all very hurtful. People who aren't divorced don't understand how difficult it is, especially when it's something you didn't choose.
>
> —Leo

All these hurtful experiences cause many divorced Catholics to flee their parishes in search of another church they can call home, usually one that will allow them to worship God in an environment that accepts them and their divorce without question or hesitation. Often they wind up joining a different parish from the one they attended before the divorce. Why? For some, their parish "home" is just a painful reminder of their divorce, and the last thing they want to do is go to church and feel alienated.

So they find another church. Sadly, in most cases they are merely compounding the losses they have already experienced with the loss of their parish family. If they have children, this compounds their sense of loss and insecurity as well. Merely escaping the discomfort and finding acceptance in a "non-judgmental atmosphere" can be a bit like slapping a Band-Aid over a deep gash: It is a temporary solution; it is not the recommended course for healing.

So, what's the solution to overcoming the stigma of divorce? This healing comes from remembering the truth about ourselves: We are precious in God's sight, and he longs to be in relationship with us. By embracing our faith and staying close to the sacraments, we can rebuild our self-worth and self-esteem, simply by staying close to the One who loves us perfectly.

Let's hear what Leo, Kara, and Grant had to say about this later in the *Voices of Hope* video:

> I have found that the Church is open and receptive to Catholics who have been through a divorce, even though I didn't think so at first. They are especially receptive in encouraging a divorced parishioner to continue coming to Mass, receiving the sacraments, and serving in the same capacity they had before. In my case, I continued to be an Extraordinary Minister of the Eucharist, a lector. By doing this, I was able to feel accepted by those people who knew me and knew my circumstances. I found that very comforting.
>
> —Leo

> My family was a huge support for me. . . . My mother helped me to see I was still important despite what had happened, and that God had chosen me as a tool for him to help other people. Through my pain, I was serving a purpose bigger than anyone knew. It made me realize the blessings I had been given, especially being chosen by God to help others. These things made me feel special, not forgotten.
>
> —Kara

> I made some conscious choices to turn away from people who were being judgmental and focus on my relationship with God. I grounded myself in my faith and found incredible healing as I opened my heart to my faith.
>
> —Grant

It is crucial to stay close to your faith and receive the sacraments frequently as you move forward. I encourage you to be patient with others in your parish or family who may be critical of your situation because they do not understand, and draw closer to the sacraments as a means of comfort and support. You will find doing this will strengthen you and help prepare you even more for a new relationship. Don't hide yourself behind the label of "divorce." Give yourself permission to let go of the stigma.

Divorce and the Catholic Parent

Another issue many divorced Catholic parents face that can help to reduce their self-esteem and confidence is the fear they may be passing on a "legacy of divorce" to their own children. This is another obstacle that can stand in the way of moving past divorce into a happy future. At one point after I remarried, I read Dr. Judith Wallerstein's groundbreaking book *The Unexpected Legacy of Divorce,* in which she chronicles her twenty-five-year study observing the effects of divorce on children as they mature. Her belief is that divorce has an exponential effect on a family:

> From the viewpoint of the children, and counter to what happens to their parents, divorce is a cumulative experience. Its impact increases over time and rises to a crescendo in adulthood. At each developmental stage divorce is experienced anew in different ways. In adulthood it affects personality, the ability to trust, expectations about relationships, and ability to cope with change.

> The children concluded early on, silently and sadly, that family relationships are fragile and that the tie between a man and woman can break capriciously, without warning. They worried ever after that parent-child relationships are also unreliable and can break at any time. These early experiences colored their later expectations.[1]

The results of Wallerstein's study are powerful and eye-opening, and they reveal precisely what many people tend to ignore in regard to the effect divorce has on children. Dismissing the trauma children experience when their parents divorce because "children are resilient" and will "bounce back" from it all is doing a grave disservice to them and to the people with whom they will later have relationships.

The truth is that children feel the same emotions adults do, in an equally powerful way, but they are incapable of expressing their feelings the way adults do. This means they carry that raw, unaddressed pain with them every day of their young lives into adulthood, where it can finally be expressed, but by then it has emotionally disfigured the child. This is why we see so many young adults strung out on illegal drugs, trapped in a cycle of self-cutting, teetering on the edge of suicide, or engaging in other immoral behaviors. Children, just as adults, need to be given ongoing opportunities to heal from their pain, such as therapy and guidance from their parents and clergy. If they are provided with these opportunities, they have a much better chance of growing up to have healthy relationships. This is why I believe handing down a legacy of failed marriages through the generations is *not* inevitable. If we don't ignore them and if we take their suffering seriously, we can help them heal and move forward to a healthy, productive life.

So, I contend that reversing generational divorce is absolutely within your control to a large degree. Of course you cannot make decisions for your grown children, but if you do everything within your control to offset the effects of the divorce now, while your children are with you, you can play a huge role in helping your child have a healthy marriage in the future.

One of the most important ways to ensure your own children will go on to have happy, healthy relationships is by working to keep your relationship and communications with your former spouse as positive and constructive as possible. As much as possible, show consideration both in how you speak to him or her in front of your children, and in how you speak *about* your ex-spouse when he or she is not around. Emotions can run high, and even if your children don't speak and act as if they love their parents, the truth is your children love both you and your ex-spouse.

For this reason, it is important to help your children maintain a loving connection with both their parents through your personal example. Speak charitably about your ex-spouse in front of your children, even if your ex-spouse refuses to reciprocate; your example will have a definite impact on your children. Whether you realize it or not, your children are watching you all the more closely since your divorce, and they are looking for truth and guidance. If they come home from spending time with your ex-spouse and have heard things that are not true, calmly and charitably give them the truth without degrading the other parent in their eyes. This may sound like an impossible suggestion, but many other single parents have practiced this type of behavior with their children, and although difficult at first, it pays off quite well in the end. This, alone, will help them in their future adult relationships as much as in their relationships with your former spouse.

What if your children are angry about your former spouse's behavior, and find it hard to maintain that relationship? Encourage your children to talk about what happened, and engage them in gentle discussions about what God intended marriage to be and about what happens when we don't live according to that plan. If you find it difficult to speak about your former spouse without anger, consider seeking the assistance of someone who can help you and your children resolve your feelings and find peace.

Reinforcing those principles of marriage and family with your children as they grow can have a tremendous, positive impact on their future relationships. If you date and eventually remarry, by following these principles in your new relationship you can actually offer a strong example of what a happy marriage looks like, mitigating the effects of the previous marriage, and thus reinforce the truth and beauty of the sacrament of marriage.

For those whose children have witnessed their divorce, the good news is that while children form their own ideas about love and marriage through their parents' example, it does not always follow that they will inevitably repeat their parents' mistakes. By learning to recognize and change unhealthy relationship patterns in their own lives, parents teach their children to take responsibility for their own choices and decisions.

For that reason, the single best and most important thing you can do to protect your children and to teach them about healthy relationships is to *take the time to properly heal from your own divorce before entering into a serious dating relationship*. By working to unload any emotional baggage, and by recognizing and working to change behaviors that contributed to the breakdown of your marriage, you will teach your children valuable lessons about what is "normal" within marriage. More importantly, as you begin dating again, you can offer your children the opportunity to see courtship as it is meant to be and shape their ideas of how they will date. These teachable moments will often improve your relationship with them as well.

Another important thing to teach your children, by example, is to base your self-worth not solely on the opinion of other people, or on your marital status, but in the knowledge that you are loved infinitely and completely by God. When we feel most unlovable, or ashamed, or alone, God is the best and most reliable source of comfort and self-affirmation. This may seem difficult or challenging at best at a time when you, yourself, are struggling to maintain your hold on these very things. How can you give all this to your children while you are working on your own makeover? You can do this with the help of others who have walked in your shoes. There are some excellent resources available for children of divorced parents that will be of great help to kids and parents:

- Lynn Cassella-Kapusinski has published numerous books for children of divorce. Her most recent book and my personal favorite for helping kids cope with their parents' breakup is *When Parents Divorce or Separate: I Can Get Through This (Catholic Guide for Kids)*. This practical workbook is an outstanding guide for children struggling to regain their own sense of self-worth and find firm footing again. It will provide excellent sources of conversation for you and your child, and an age-appropriate clarification for your child about what happened to the family.
- Dr. Ross Campbell's series of *How to Really Love Your Child* books (. . . *Your Angry Child, Your Teen,* etc.) are excellent guides based on Christian principles for

helping your child cope. These books are used and recommended by many Catholic therapists.

- CatholicTherapists.com, founded by Allison Riccardi, is a fantastic website where you can search for a solid Catholic therapist in your area. Therapy is a great way to help kids start talking about their pain and they often feel more comfortable with an adult that is not their parent because they don't have to worry about hurting Mom's or Dad's feelings with what they want to say. Many of these therapists take phone appointments and you can find one who specifically treats children of divorce. It is so important to keep elements of your Catholic faith in the therapeutic process and this site makes access to these types of therapists easy.

I highly recommend taking advantage of these resources to help you and your children heal as much as possible and regain your self-worth, which leads us to another important discussion point . . .

Can I Still Receive Communion?

One of the greatest, most important gifts you can give yourself and your children is to remain close to Jesus in his healing Eucharistic presence as you begin this new stage of your family life. Take your children with you to spend time in front of the Blessed Sacrament, praying together as a family for an increase of love and forgiveness. Go to confession regularly to help you break spiritually toxic habits that so easily develop in times of stress and pain. Most importantly, continue to receive the Eucharist to strengthen and console you in times of loneliness and uncertainty. Know that God is always reaching out to you, even when you cannot feel his presence in your life. He is waiting patiently to be with you and to hear everything that is on your heart.

Perhaps you didn't realize that a divorce, in and of itself, does not prevent you from receiving the Eucharist. Anyone in a state of grace (who has not committed a mortal sin since their last confession) is encouraged to receive this sacrament. The confusion over this issue has to do with those Catholics who have been divorced and civilly remarried. A civilly remarried Catholic may not receive the sacraments until he or she goes through the annulment process and receives a decree of nullity. Why? Because the Church considers all marriages to be valid unless proven otherwise by the annulment process.

Many people who don't understand the reason for the Church's teaching believe it is harsh and discriminatory to deny the Eucharist to divorced Catholics who have remarried without an annulment. Some regard the "right" to receive Communion as a sort of "human rights" issue, as though this restriction treats divorced and civilly remarried Catholics unfairly, like second-class citizens.

In fact, nothing could be farther from the truth. What is true, is that anyone—married, never married, widowed, divorced, religious—who is not in the state of grace is prohibited from receiving Holy Communion. As we read in the *Catechism of the Catholic Church*: "To respond to this invitation we must prepare ourselves for so great and so holy a moment. . . . Anyone conscious of a grave sin must receive the sacrament of Reconciliation before coming to communion" (CCC 1385). So, it's not only divorced and civilly remarried Catholics who cannot receive the Eucharist; it is any Catholic who is outside the state of grace.

From the earliest times, the fathers of the Church took seriously the issue of approaching the Eucharist in a worthy manner. They did not simply overlook sin but urged the faithful to put things right before approaching the table of the Lord. In the fourth century St. John Chrysostom, one of the early fathers of the Church, urged Christians to approach the Eucharist properly disposed, not just with clean hands and clean clothes but with clean souls: "You dare not touch the host with dirty hands, even if grave necessity urged you. Likewise, do not approach the Eucharist with a dirty soul, because that would be much graver and carries with it a more terrible punishment."[2]

In a homily he gave on Christmas Day, this great saint further preached the necessity of being properly disposed: "When you approach the awesome and divine table (altar) and those sacred mysteries, do it with fear and trembling, with a clear conscience, with prayer and fasting. Do not approach in disorder . . . that would show great arrogance and no small disrespect. . . . Man, think to yourself what a great Victim you are going to touch, what table you are approaching. Consider that you being earth and ashes, take the blood and body of Christ."[3]

When we approach the Eucharist, this holy miracle right in front of us, we must prepare ourselves to receive with a humble and grateful heart. The Eucharist is healing medicine for those who struggle to overcome sin, and because we all are in need of this medicine, let there be nothing standing in the way of our ability to partake in it. Just as it is necessary to discern what happened in our first marriage in order to be free to enter fully into marriage a second time, so we must deal with any serious sin on our hearts before we approach Jesus in the Eucharist, in order to fully and honestly receive all the graces he wants to give us there.

If we are living in a way that is contrary to what the Church teaches, it inevitably distances us from God. And just as it is a serious sin to have sexual intimacy without the sacramental bond of matrimony, so it is a sin to seek out the spiritual intimacy of receiving the Eucharist when we have serious sin in our lives. God knows our hearts; he sees how far our hearts are from him.

For all these reasons, the Church teaches that those who have committed any serious sin must not receive the Eucharist. It is a way to protect her children and preserve the necessary respect for the Eucharist. This mandate is not intended to ostracize *you;* it is about protecting you and encouraging you to face the reality of your situation, confess any wrongdoing in order to resolve your circumstances, and receive the Eucharist worthily.

What should you do if you know that you have made choices that are spiritually harmful to yourself and others, and want to make things right with God? Fortunately, God does not leave us to our own devices when we sin! The sacrament of reconciliation is there for anyone who wants to make a fresh start. Make an appointment with your pastor to discuss it with him. The Church is not a hotel for saints, it is said; it is a hospital for sinners. We all need to avail ourselves of the healing graces that are there for the taking!

Rediscovering Your Self Worth

In the Gospel of Matthew (19:3–12) and again in Mark (10:2–12), Jesus teaches on the reality of divorce as something outside of God's original plan for men and women. The reason for this is simple: because he loves us, he wants everything that is good for us. God doesn't want us to suffer the deep wounds that result from divorce, wounds that so easily damage a person's self-worth. He knows that divorce can produce deep-seated emotional wounds that make it difficult for many people to find love again, and may cause them to go on in life feeling less valuable as a person. My friend, don't fall into this trap!

Let's explore the qualities that make a person truly loving and lovable. Our personal value *must not* be measured by what other people think of us. Our value as human beings is given to us by God and affirmed by the lives we live. When we are open and affectionate, when we embrace and live out our faith in generous service to others, we become the most attractive versions of ourselves.

Think about people you consider attractive. What they likely share in common is a kind of confidence that comes from this sense of self-worth. They do not define or limit themselves according to the circumstances of their lives. In most cases, their focus is not inward, but outward—interacting with others in ways that are positive and affirming.

Similarly, if you want to elevate your level of attractiveness, remember you are *not* defined by a mere word. "Divorce" does not and could never encapsulate who you are as a person. You are a living, breathing human being with a mind and a body, a heart and a soul. You are loved by a God who created you and gave you a distinct purpose in life. You are not the sum of one word, nor are you validated by a social status.

Divorce is something that happened to you.
It is not who you are.

Divorce does not invalidate your role as an important family member, friend, or member of society. It does not erase all the good qualities you possess or all the good things you've done. It certainly does not negate all the incredible potential you have for living the rest of your life. Believing this is critical if you hope to have a successful relationship in the future. In fact, despite the trauma of the situation and the dramatic ways in which your life has changed, your divorce is still a relatively small part of who you are in the grand scheme of things. It certainly is not the way God defines you. When you doubt your own self-worth, it's appropriate and necessary to step back once in a while and give yourself a reality check.

> So we do not lose heart.
> Even though our outer nature is wasting away,
> our inner nature is being renewed day by day.
> For this slight momentary affliction is preparing us
> for an eternal weight of glory beyond all measure,
> because we look not at what can be seen but at what cannot be seen;
> for what can be seen is temporary, but what cannot be seen is eternal.
>
> —2 Corinthians 4:16–18

As you do the due diligence of healing and preparation that is necessary after divorce, you will rediscover your self-worth; all the incredible gifts and talents God has already given you are waiting to be refreshed and refined as well as your ability to see how precious you are in his sight. Not only will your life begin to be happy again, but you will see you are capable of having a healthy, thriving, and exciting romantic relationship, if that is the road you choose to take.

You will find it helpful to keep in mind these specific truths as you move forward:

- You are a human being with the potential to do great things.
- You are loved by God so much so that he came down to earth and died on the Cross for you. If you were the only person on earth, he would do it again—*for you.*

He has bestowed many gifts and talents upon you, and has given you a distinct purpose in life.

Now What?

God has given you—just as he has given each one of us—a distinct purpose, a mission that is as unique and unrepeatable as snowflakes or fingerprints. If you are able to recognize and embrace the fact that you are not just a number, not just a statistic, but someone with a unique identity and a specific purpose in life, you will emanate a new level of attractiveness that so many people miss out on, especially those who have lowered their expectations in life because of their divorce experience. They are content to just "get by" in life. They haven't opened their eyes to the truth that they were born with a purpose. Instead, they just live to survive.

Here is your opportunity to step beyond that mentality and infuse your attractiveness with a sense of purpose. Never doubt that, although you are one among many, God has graced you with gifts, talents, and a temperament that are all unique to you. It is no mistake you were born at this particular time in history to your particular parents in the particular city in which you were born. It is not an accident you come from your specific ethnic background or that you are a Christian. All of it is intentional on God's part, and he gave you all this because he wants you to put it to good use. If you use these gifts and talents—develop them to their full potential—you will experience life in an incredible way.

Discover Your Purpose

About halfway through my post-divorce single years, I became aware of the obstacles that were standing in the way of being happy, and I became committed to doing whatever was necessary to overcome them. It was hard to do because I had become comfortable in my sadness, in being a bit of a hermit and not being very social, so it meant I really had to push myself out of my comfort zone. I needed to get comfortable doing things I wasn't comfortable doing. To begin, I needed to get out more. I needed to go places and do things even if it meant doing them alone until I had friends or dates with whom I could share these experiences.

One day, I decided I would take a day trip to Manhattan and visit the Metropolitan Museum of Art. Once inside this awesome place, I was grateful I had made myself come. It was incredible to witness centuries of masterful art in all its various forms. But there was one painting in particular that swept me up and mesmerized me. I must have stared at it for at least twenty minutes because it was so captivating. It was the oil painting of Joan of Arc by Jules Bastien-Lepage (French, Damvillers 1848–1884 Paris). I felt so connected to the woman in that painting . . . a young Joan looking off to the distance, knowing she had a mission to fulfill and longing to embark on that mission. The painting also depicts Saints Michael, Margaret, and Catherine rousing her to follow her calling . . . what a magnificent feeling it was to share that same wonderment with her and the artist who so beautifully painted it.

You might share these sentiments, too. Maybe, you've assumed you were already fulfilling your mission when you were married, but your divorce has taken that away from you, and now you don't know what your purpose is. Don't give in to the idea that you have lost your purpose because of what has happened. There is no time like the present to focus on discerning your new direction and purpose in life. Dating can help you discern this.

At this point in your life, dating will become a process of helping you grow into your new identity and learn about yourself in new ways. It will help you discover what God wants you to do with your life from this point forward . . . are you meant to remarry? Could there be other options out there for you? As we continue through these pages, we will discover just how important social relationships are to discerning your new path. You even have a purpose as you go through this discernment stage that I like to call a "mini-mission": a smaller, focused accomplishment for a certain period of time.

As we discussed before, you have many gifts from God, your time included, and he wants you to use these gifts wisely. What could you be doing as a single person to help fulfill your mini-mission?

When I was in this period of my life, I fulfilled two mini-missions that really helped move me forward in rebuilding my life and keeping my attitude positive; I went through the approval process for Big Brothers / Big Sisters and became a Big Sister to a sweet little girl in need. I also became a CCD teacher at my parish. Both of these helped draw me outside of myself and focus on others, an exercise I highly recommend. *What could you be doing at this time?*

♥

> Each of us has a specific purpose in life. Every soul is called to a unique mission that only they can fulfill. This is our Father's amazing plan for each one of his children, intricately designed so that all of us who cooperate with his will can be happy in this life and supremely happy with him forever in heaven.
>
> Our Lord's greatest desire for you is to become a saint, to be holy. In 2 Timothy 1:9 Saint Paul says, "For God saved us and called us to live a holy life. he did this not because we deserve it, but because it was his plan from the beginning of time, to show us his grace through Jesus Christ."
>
> —Tom Peterson
> Founder and president of Catholics Come Home, Inc.

♥

Let's Get Started

There is no time like the present to get started on identifying and implementing some of these resolutions and begin moving forward. This next step is a very important part of preparing yourself for a new relationship or whatever the future holds, because it involves examining your own ideas and expectations about your self-worth, love, dating, and marriage.

Traumatic, life-changing situations like a divorce often cause us to rethink our stance on important personal issues. In my experience, I began doubting the good things about myself I already knew were true, and didn't realize how much it affected my expectations and the way I interacted with other people. Here is a chance for you to take an objective look at what you believe to be true about yourself.

Write down your thoughts as you read. An important part of this exercise is stepping outside yourself as much as possible for a more objective viewpoint, which is why I strongly encourage you to begin using a journal. Getting these thoughts and ideas out of your head and onto paper will not only provide you with a cathartic experience but also help you assess yourself more objectively. Don't use one you have already started for some other project or purpose; use something totally new and completely dedicated to this process.

Whether you put some loose-leaf sheets in a three-ring binder or purchase something elaborate to write in makes no difference, as long as it suits you and makes you want to use it. Just make sure you have some way to record your answers to the examinations and questionnaires you will find in this book, and to write down any other thoughts that occur to you as you read. I've done this many, many times, myself; I can confidently assure you that your journal will become a therapeutic tool as well as an accurate indicator of the progress you will make. One day in the future, you will pick it up again, read it, and be absolutely amazed at the progress you have made. You will be able to see how God has worked in your life.

Use the "quizzes" in each chapter to track your progress. This first questionnaire is intended to help you gain a basic idea of how you view yourself, and the second will illuminate your views and ideas of dating and marriage. This will be a great opportunity for you to make an honest observation of where you stand.

Quiz: "How Do I See Myself?"

Answer these questions on a separate sheet of paper using this key:

1=Definitely 2=Sort of 3=Not at all

1. I am capable of having a good relationship.
2. A new relationship is the key to healing.
3. Starting to date again is the only thing that will help me to feel better about myself.
4. I often feel devastated or depressed.
5. I have difficulty trusting others in a reasonable way.
6. Someone who loves me makes me feel validated.
7. I have stopped replaying the negative events of my divorce in my mind.
8. I have learned to interact peacefully with my ex-spouse.
9. I deserve it when someone mistreats me.
10. What I look like is the most important "attraction factor."

11. I know I am loved if my partner wants to have sex.
12. I am worthy of being loved.
13. I tend to magnify my mistakes and minimize my successes.
14. I am critical of others in an unfair manner.
15. Sexual intimacy is okay after divorce.
16. I am at peace with my divorce.
17. I am a positive influence on others.
18. I make decisions primarily based on what would make others happy.
19. I have a definite set of goals for my future.
20. All in all, I am inclined to feel that I am a failure.
21. I feel I do not have much to be proud of.
22. I take a positive attitude toward myself.
23. On the whole, I am satisfied with myself.
24. I often deserve it when others treat me with disrespect.
25. At times I think I am no good at all.

Now, take a look at your score. Numbers 1, 7, 8, 12, 16, 17, 19, 22, and 23 are all questions that should be answered as "definitely." All the rest should be "not at all." What does this indicate about your readiness to date? Your answers reveal how valuable you feel as a person and either how much your divorce has stolen that from you and must be restored or how much work you've already done in this area and have emerged from your divorce with a healthy sense of self-worth.

If only a few of your answers were different, focus on correcting those ideas, but all in all, you should be able to begin moving forward with no problem.

If you had different responses to four or more of the questions, it may be time to step back from the idea of dating to find a serious relationship for a while and start working on the areas that are holding you back. Avoid making your first dating mistake: moving forward believing you are less attractive, less worthy, and less lovable because of your divorce. This frame of mind is not conducive to having a healthy relationship.

Of course, you still need relationships with other people. This is not the time to stay home alone and forgo any type of social interaction—definitely not. Social relationships play a huge role in your healing process. But, instead of jumping into a heavy romantic relationship that will most likely lead you to making more mistakes, let these social relationships help you heal and bring you the joy of being with other people.

On the other hand, acknowledging these personal issues and taking action to correct them before you invest your heart in a serious dating relationship is a courageous step, one you will be very happy you took and one that will pay off for you in big ways. At the end of this book you will find an appendix containing a list of recommended reading to help you with specific areas of concern. I also recommend seeking spiritual direction from a solid Catholic priest and spending time in eucharistic adoration as often as your schedule permits. Time with Christ in the Blessed Sacrament provides fulfillment and peace, no matter what the rest of your life looks like. In my own personal experience, eucharistic adoration has always been a beacon of peace and understanding in my life, tethering me to Christ in a way only the Eucharist can.

Now, the Five Attraction Factors

In the chapters that follow, we're going to look at five qualities that are found in every attractive person. They may express these qualities in different ways or to different degrees depending on their personality and upon the nature of the relationship. These five qualities are:

- Being *available,*
- Being *affectionate,*
- Being a *communicator,*
- Being *faithful,* and
- Being *magnanimous.*

When these factors are cultivated, you naturally become the best, most attractive version of yourself, someone other people want to be near, someone with whom people want to form stronger attachments. Whether or not you decide you are ready to date seriously or just date socially, you can work on these attraction factors with those around you every day. If you ask him, God will assist you in strengthening these attraction factors through his graces.

A Reflection on the Heart of Christ

In every situation we encounter in life, it is good to remember that while Jesus was on earth, he encountered the same struggles and challenges we do. It is always appropriate to look at his earthly life and see what we can glean from his example so we can use it as guidance and inspiration as we forge ahead. In speaking in terms of getting ready to love again, we can note that Christ went through a very similar process. He lived thirty-three years, and only three of those years were spent in public ministry. The rest of the time he spent preparing for the time in which he would show everyone he encountered how to love.

"As the Father loves me, so I also love you. Remain in my love. I have told you this so that my joy may be in you and your joy may be complete. It was not you who chose me, but I who chose you and appointed you to go and bear fruit that will remain so that whatever you ask the Father in my name He may give you. This I command you: Love one another" (Jn 15:9, 11, 16–17). These words from the New Testament reveal the depths of God's love for us, and also, his plan for us. His love for us is so great, so perfect, and he wants us not only to receive it, but also to pass it on to those whom we encounter. That is why this time of preparation is so important, and in the future when you look back at this period of your life, you will understand just how meaningful it is.

What a great gift we have been given in being chosen by Christ to love others. As you move forward, if you ever doubt what you are doing or feel discouraged, come back to this passage and re-read his words, for in them you will find the comfort, motivation, and inspiration he wants to give you.

Questions for Reflection

1. Am I still struggling with the stigma of being divorced? If so, is it rooted in feeling I am not lovable or worthy? In what ways does this play out in my life right now?
2. My divorce is an experience that happened to me, not something that defines me. Have I accepted this truth and assimilated it into my way of thinking? Why or why not?

3. Do I feel lovable and worthy of being loved? If not, what are the reasons why I feel this way? How can I change this?
4. What kind of people am I surrounding myself with? Are these relationships likely to help me discern God's purposes for my life?
5. Am I currently invested in any relationships that do not bring out the best in me? What do I need to do to free myself from the effects of these relationships, and make room for healthier relationships?
6. During this period of being single, what are some possible things I can do to fulfill my mini-mission?

Next Steps

Here are some practical suggestions for implementing the points and suggestions in this chapter:

- Make a list of your good qualities and talents and bring it with you the next time you go to Mass, where you can offer them up in thanksgiving and pray for the grace to use them well.
- Consider following up on any items you missed in the "How Do I See Myself?" quiz with a confessor, spiritual director, or therapist.
- Take some time to evaluate your friendships to see if some action needs to be taken.
- Explore opportunities available to you to serve others and accomplish a mini-mission.

Chapter Two

Being Available

The first attraction factor we are going to discuss is *being available*. It may seem like a contradiction in terms: You are divorced from your ex-spouse so how is it you are not available? There are several things to consider here. Allow me to share a little more of my story with you to help explain.

Can I Date?

I sat across from Fr. Joe in his office, a broken woman. It had been two horrific months since my husband had asked for a divorce and walked out, and this compassionate priest in his late forties had been the voice of reason and sanity for me during that time. "What was I going to do? How would I cope? Could I still come to Mass? Would I be able to receive the sacraments?"

All of these questions and many more were the subjects of the spiritual direction he gave me. Fr. Joe was solid in his faith and knowledge of Church teaching, and he also held a degree in psychology. He had dispensed a lot of realistic, practical advice and I trusted him. So it only made sense to bring up another equally important question I had.

"Can I date?"

"Yes. I don't see any reason why you can't."

This was not the answer I had expected. It seemed like it shouldn't be that easy, but his words to me did bring a sense of relief. Many of my friends at work had been hounding me to go out on a date, partly because they were tired of seeing me sad and depressed. I always refused on principle. I didn't want to date someone else; I wanted to be married to my husband! You know, the one who was supposed to love me "till death do us part"? How could being with someone I didn't love be good when I still loved my husband?

This quandary was the bane of my existence. But as time wore on and I witnessed my soon-to-be ex-husband move on immediately and with such great ease, I began to rethink my position.

I was furious he had left me for someone else, and I began to think going on a date would be good for me. Maybe being with someone who thought I was attractive and interesting would put me in a better mood? I wonder how he'll feel when he sees me out with someone else. He'll be jealous. I'll be happy.

When a coworker asked me out just a few days later, I accepted. We dated several times and before I knew it I was floating on a cloud . . . excited, happy, and literally consumed with the incredible feeling that someone found me special and attractive. I was totally hooked.

And yet, it did not take me long to realize that dating to spite my ex-spouse was very likely the worst possible reason to date. What I didn't understand until it was too late and I was in over my head was that my date just wanted to have fun, not a long-term relationship. I wish I could say it all ended well, but I can't. It ended badly, as did many of the mini-relationships I got into after my divorce. Each time one ended, I was left feeling more hurt than the time before and less trusting of the opposite sex. It piled layer upon layer of pain on the open wound of my divorce. This was no way to live, and I had to find a different answer.

♥

> Most relationships, especially second and third marriages, fail because of contraception, and I'm not talking pills. People who have lost everything in a prior divorce or had their hearts chewed up and spit out often enter new relationships with an equal mix of anticipation and fear—ready for the pleasure and perks but afraid of being used, hurt, and deprived of things. Never again! So they put invisible "condoms" on their hearts, wallets, property, and even their time. They are protected but such is not love. It's just another form of using the other person and protecting the self. No true life can spring forth from such a thwarted attempt at union.
>
> —Rose Sweet, author of *Rebuilding After Divorce*

♥

Why Dating Didn't Help Me

As I looked back on that conversation with Fr. Joe years later, I realized something important. Although the answer I got from him was "technically" correct, it was problematic in practice. He was technically correct because there is nothing in canon law or the *Catechism of the Catholic Church* that specifically prohibits one from dating after a divorce. I have scoured canon law in search of some reference to this and have also discussed the issue with several canon lawyers. The only across-the-board mandate regarding a new relationship after a divorce comes from a tribunal at the beginning of the annulment process which states no plans for a new marriage can be made before a final decree of nullity is received. In some nullity cases the tribunal places a prohibition for remarriage on one or both of the parties because there may be psychological issues that need to be addressed or an attitude not in keeping with important aspects of marriage. But those address remarriage, not dating. I believe many people who are not ready to date, as was the case for me, are given the green light to do so anyway based on this technicality.

This leads many divorced Catholics to believe sincerely their next best step is to go out and find another serious relationship, and that finding someone new will help them get over the pain of their divorces and find happiness once again. But in practice, jumping right back into a serious relationship after a divorce can create some real problems, and for several reasons:

Reason #1: All marriages are considered to be valid/sacramental unless proven otherwise by the annulment process. So in my case, as an example, although I had a civil divorce decree and my union with my ex-spouse was dissolved in the eyes of the state, the Church still considered me to be married. Only a decree of nullity (annulment) could determine whether a valid / sacramental bond existed between my ex-spouse and me.

Reason #2: There are no shortcuts to healing. I was not healed at all from my divorce, and I was using dating and intimacy as a sort of pain reliever *and* as a way to spite my ex-spouse. *I was using men for my own gratification,* not respecting them, and that is unhealthy for anyone involved in a relationship.

Reason #3: The wounded heart attaches easily. Trying to form an attachment before the heart is strong and ready for that kind of commitment only compounds the woundedness. That is why so many people go from relationship to relationship without ever finding that peace and fulfillment they seek.

I believe these are important points to consider before you begin dating because, again, the goal is to set you on a path to happiness, and if you enter into a relationship prematurely, before your heart is prepared to give and receive love again, you run the risk of making some very painful mistakes.

Case in point: A recently divorced gentleman decided it was time to get back out there and start dating. The loss of his marriage had devastated him, but he was consoled by the fact that his two children would be living with him. He met a woman who seemed to be in very much the same predicament; they exchanged phone numbers and talked for hours. Within a matter of months, they proclaimed the joyful news of their engagement. They wanted to get married right away and, despite the reaction from family and friends—all who tried to talk them out of such an impulsive move—that is exactly what happened. They moved in together and began the process of integrating their already broken-hearted children into a new family, which is not an easy thing to do.

They got divorced less than a year later.

I share that with you to illustrate why it is critical to be properly prepared for a new relationship. Emotions may be powerful, but they are not reliable and do not provide the common sense necessary to make sound decisions. Who wants to go through another divorce? If you fall in love again, wouldn't you want it to be spectacular? Wouldn't you want to give that relationship as much hope of succeeding as possible? This is why it is so important to do the necessary work to make sure you are *completely* available.

In light of that, there are just two more points I would like to offer for your consideration:

1. Consider Reconciliation

One afternoon in September of 1993, I sat in my car in the parking lot of the local Denny's restaurant working up the nerve to make a very gutsy move—I was going to ask my estranged spouse to consider reconciliation instead of divorce. It had been like pulling teeth to get him to agree to meet me, especially since I did not tell him why I wanted to see him. And I normally would have labeled myself as insane for doing something so bold, especially when I believed I already knew what his answer would be, but something inside was pushing me forward.

Proposing that we try to save our marriage would not be easy for me; there was no question about that. I had been betrayed and abandoned, and asking him to give our marriage another chance admittedly made me look like the weaker party, as if I was emotionally unable to let go of a relationship that was over. The thought of doing this was painful and humiliating, but *it was still something I knew I had to do.*

I walked into the restaurant with my heart pounding so hard I thought I would have a heart attack. Would I be able to go through with this? After keeping me waiting for fifteen minutes, he finally showed up. I nearly lost my nerve because of how much he had visibly changed. It was like a switch had been flipped; the man I had married was gone. In his stead was a cold man, someone I didn't recognize at all.

In the end, my efforts proved to be fruitless, and the actual conversation was even more devastating than the day he left. Yet, I have *never* regretted taking that risk and asking him to consider reconciliation. I believe it was the right thing for me to do, and I encourage anyone not living in an abusive or dangerous marriage relationship to consider taking this same step.

By giving God a chance to work in your spouse's heart, and through your willingness to risk loving even when it hurts, the graces you've received as a married couple are activated and have the opportunity to produce good fruit. Of course, it takes the free will of both spouses to cooperate with those graces, and that doesn't always happen, but just think of what could happen if you both did . . . Just opening this door can lead to some amazing things. It is possible for a couple to reconcile after such deep hurt.

Let's survey the landscape on this one for a moment. It is possible you might not be in a position to ask your ex-spouse for reconciliation. Maybe your ex-spouse is already remarried, or maybe the circumstances that led to the separation (abuse or violence or other lifestyle choices) dictate that it really is too late to reconcile. There may be some circumstances, however, when reconciliation is possible if both spouses are willing to swallow their pride and start over. I can think of two good reasons for this:

Reason #1: Divorce tends to create more problems than it solves. A period of separation of the spouses can cause one to rethink one's decision, regret the divorce, and silently long for reconciliation. When one spouse steps forward in humility instead of anger and indignation, the possibilities broaden. Acts of humility have the potential to soften even the hardest of hearts.

Reason #2: Even if your spouse declines to reconcile, it won't be a wasted effort. If your marriage cannot be saved and your spouse declines your request, taking that courageous step can still be very healing for you. You will never look back years later and wonder, *what if*? Knowing I did all I could to save my marriage was extremely healing for me, and when I remarried after going through the annulment process, I had no hesitation whatsoever.

If you decide to take this step, some people may try to talk you out of it. I had a few people who knew I was going to ask my ex-spouse for reconciliation frown upon this decision, saying it would be "psychologically healthier" for me if I just let go of my spouse and went my own way. They questioned the sanity of wanting to go back to a spouse who had so blatantly betrayed me. But I wanted a clear conscience, and taking this step gave me that benefit.

Society doesn't value the virtue of humility anymore, and this makes the idea of asking for reconciliation sound like the wrong idea. An eye for an eye is the law of the land. On the other hand, Christ reminds us to go the extra mile, to offer not just our coat and hat but our shirt as well (see Matthew 5:38–42). No matter how ridiculous it may seem to other people, your decision to ask your spouse for reconciliation has nothing to do with them, nor do they have the right to try and stop you. They may tell you you're humiliating yourself, but you are actually humbling yourself if you approach it with sincerity. That is a *huge* difference.

2. Take Advantage of the Annulment Process

There are so many myths and misconceptions about the Catholic annulment process, which make many people decide they want nothing to do with it. I find this very sad because there is so much opportunity for healing that is being missed. True, the annulment process is only obligatory if you want to get married again, but it is important not to look at this as just a means to a particular end, something you have to do if you want to remarry. There is so much to gain from going through with it, if you approach it with a heart that is open to seeking God's will and desires healing. Some of the benefits of this process are:

- *It will help you to take a bold and honest look at yourself.* Systematically examining what happened in your dating relationship, engagement, and marriage—and to accept the truth about what happened—will help you. Being able to admit that both spouses made mistakes and bad decisions, even if one spouse cheated or abandoned the family, takes a lot of courage because so many people today have a victim mentality and blame all the bad things that happen to them on someone else. And yet, a victim is never happy. A victim will never experience real personal growth. It takes humility to admit your mistakes, especially mistakes that cause something so devastating as a divorce. That being said, taking a hard look at what happened and accepting whatever role you played in the demise of your marriage becomes a source of humility, strength, and peace of heart.
- *It helps you to learn from your mistakes.* You gain wisdom through experiencing the trials of life, fighting your way through them, and coming out the other side where you can look back and see it all from a different perspective. The annulment process helps you do this as it lays out the "big picture" for you so you can understand what happened in your relationship with your former spouse in a more objective way. In doing so, it also prepares you for making better choices the next time around.
- *It provides an opportunity for spiritual growth.* At a time in your life when trust in others is typically at an all-time low, it is important to turn to God for answers and guidance. God wants you to trust him with every part of your life, and to come to him with all your cares, worries, concerns, hopes, dreams, and desires. But just asking for help is not what builds trust; believing that he will take care of you and work these circumstances for your good is the way to build that trust. The annulment process

helps with this because after you have provided your explanation of what happened and all other testimonies are gathered, the ultimate decision is in the hands of the tribunal and it usually takes a while to receive it. This is an opportunity to place your trust in God's plan and pray for the canon lawyers who will make the final determination.

- *It enables you to regain complete confidence in the direction you take in life.* By the time you receive your decision, you have been able to close this chapter of your life and lay it aside so you can embark on a completely new chapter. No matter what decision the tribunal returns—whether you are free to marry or are still considered married—you now have a clear direction to take with many possibilities to find happiness.

If you are wrestling with the decision to go through the annulment process, I encourage you to talk to your pastor or spiritual director about it. Give yourself the gift of time, to ensure you have done the hard work you need to do to fully heal from your divorce. I will always be thankful for everything I learned about myself and my expectations of marriage through the annulment process and receiving that decree of nullity. It absolutely prepared me for my new marriage, to ensure that I was truly *available* to enter into another relationship with the blessing of the Church! Whether or not you decide to get married again, an incredible experience awaits you as you discover the most reliable source of healing, found in God and the Church—the place we can experience the perfect, healing love of Jesus.

Turn Your Pain into Passion

Are you still feeling the pain of your divorce, even though you thought by now it would be different? That is totally normal. Because divorce is a traumatic event, you will always feel some sort of pain associated with memories of your divorce, although the sting will dull and fade as time goes by. Someday in the future when your life is very happy, something will remind you of the past . . . a song, a movie, an old memento, meeting someone who resembles your ex-spouse, etc., and it will hurt. You may even shed a tear. But it shouldn't ruin your day or affect you to the point you cannot continue what you are doing at that moment. Melancholy memories that come crashing back into your thought process are normal, but becoming paralyzed by them ten years down the road is not. A great way to deal with the suffering is by channeling this lingering pain into passion.

Passion is a word originated in Latin, and literally means "to suffer." Although this word has taken on quite a different meaning these days, the original definition was *the willing suffering of Christ*. Currently, *passion* has become synonymous with *pleasure* and what people find exciting or adventurous. But because it is originally defined as the moment of the deepest willing suffering of Christ for our good, it is intended to describe the transcendence of human desires to a love that is willing to suffer. So, in turning your pain into passion, it means during this time in your life where you still feel the painful effects of your divorce, a time that is temporary, you resolve to live it in a way that gives meaning to your suffering.

For example, you can offer your pain to God in prayer for specific intentions such as for couples who are on the brink of divorce, or someone you know who is struggling with depression or other health issues. You can allow the pain to motivate you to develop a virtuous habit—for instance, maybe in your marriage you had a habit of arguing a point to death because you had an unquenchable need to be right all the time. Instead of just feeling bad about what happened, you can allow those painful memories to motivate you to work on being more humble. The point is to use the pain in a positive way, and in doing so you will find the pain not only helps you develop a more positive attitude but fades more quickly, too.

This is not the way many other people think, unfortunately. People don't like to be in pain, especially when the suffering is prolonged. And, since it isn't possible to just pop an aspirin and make that pain go away, people look for other ways to soothe their suffering. Most often that is looking for a romantic relationship with someone who will make them feel attractive, interesting, and loveable again. Because emotion is fueling this search for relief from pain, it is rather dangerous to get involved with someone at this point, similar to a drunk driver getting behind the wheel of a car.

On the flip side of that coin, you have the well-meaning but misguided "help" of friends, family, and coworkers who urge you to dive back into the dating pool before you are ready to swim. Just as people don't like to be in pain, people also don't like to watch others suffer. People who observe others who are in pain or enduring emotional suffering usually react to it with some level of uneasiness. They want that person's suffering to stop, and they want to help fix the problem in some way, but the problem is out of their control. This makes them uncomfortable and awkward. So, they actively encourage their loved one to get back out there and start dating again as their way of helping to stop the suffering. Their efforts to get you out there are probably very sincere, of course, but it isn't the right kind of advice if your heart is not truly available.

Instead of trying to ease the pain through dating, turn that pain into passion and remember that suffering has a cleansing effect to it because it can breed virtuous habits and bring you out of yourself to focus on others. Suffering helps you improve and become a better person, if you allow it to.

Walking Through the Fire

By our very nature, we fall and we get back up. We make a mistake and we start over, but wiser because of the mistake. Trials and challenges serve specifically to strengthen and purify us. Even in sacred scripture, we have many descriptions of God as the refiner who purifies his people through fire just as silver and gold are purified. So what is most important about the suffering we face is not getting rid of it or trying to avoid it; it is learning from it and allowing it to change us into a better person.

Here are a few suggestions to help you detach from it and find the real path to healing:

- *Give yourself the gift of time.* Slow down and take time to reflect upon the things you want to change. After you have done that, take some time to write those things down; then, write down how you will make those changes. This provides you with concrete steps to begin effecting a positive change.
- *Make prayer a simple conversation with God.* I found praying this way a great comfort . . . speaking to him just as I would a trusted friend and asking for strength to do what needed to be done. Have you ever noticed how children go through life, trusting their parents and other adults for everything! They trust we will feed them good food, protect them from harm, take them fun places, and buy them good things. Why should you trust him any less? He knows best what will make you happy. Christ

is calling you to return to him, come closer to him. Open your heart to him and resolve to take a step closer to him each day.

- *Keep your eyes on the goal*. Trust God to take care of you. The best way to handle the pain of divorce is by facing it, not running from it or putting a lid on it. Facing this kind of suffering takes a great deal of courage because it requires accepting the loss with humility, forgiving those who have hurt you, and admitting the truth about mistakes that were made on the part of both spouses. Take the steps you need to take to detach from what is holding you back. When the temptation to do the things you know will divert you from your goal present themselves, say a quick prayer for strength (God, help me!) and remind yourself why you set this goal.

An important aspect of taking these steps is making sure you surround yourself with people who will help you to become the best and most attractive versions of yourself. At some point you need to stop and ask: Are the people I am surrounding myself with holding me back from having a healthy perspective on my future? Are they possibly keeping me from finding someone special? It is something to take note of because oftentimes our friends, coworkers, and even family members can keep us heading in one direction when we should be heading in another.

I encourage you to pray about these things and ask God to lead you in the direction of good and healthy relationships. Ask for the grace to know if you should be taking action in any particular way to make this happen.

The Five Keys to Healing

Healing from divorce takes time, patience, and personal reflection, but there will come a point when you *know* you are ready to date. There are many opinions about exactly how much time it takes, but the truth is, it's different for everyone. However, there are some practical, concrete steps you can act on right away that will move you down that path much faster. These steps are what I refer to as the *Five Keys to Healing*.

Key #1: Acceptance

Divorce, especially for the spouse who was abandoned, creates a slippery slope, the blame game. I played the blame game, myself, for quite a while after my divorce. I blamed many people for what had happened before, during, and after my divorce: my ex-spouse, the "other women," my in-laws, God, etc. The blame game transformed me into a victim, and in playing it, I was actually avoiding the truth about my situation. I needed to stop blaming and start accepting.

What did I have to accept? I had to accept my marriage was over and, as much as I wanted to, there was no way I could change that. This was an agonizing revelation for me and a difficult one to accept. It took me a while to admit how much I was still hoping for reconciliation, and having to accept it wouldn't happen was tough. There was no marriage anymore. My hands were completely tied when it came to my ex-husband's actions, attitudes, and excuses he gave others for our divorce. He didn't love me and was doing things to hurt me. I had to accept that and learn to move forward. I also had to accept that I, too, carried some of the blame for the divorce. I was always faithful to my husband and tried to be a good wife, but the reality was I wasn't perfect and my many mistakes contributed to the divorce.

These were all difficult steps to take, but once I took them, I made progress. This important exercise in accepting the truth made it easier to pray and be at peace. I still didn't understand why it all happened, but I had come to a place where I could stop blaming God and turned to him for strength instead. I encourage you to take your time with this step.

Key #2: Forgiveness

C. S. Lewis probably said it best: "Forgiveness is like monkey bars; you have to let go in order to move forward,"[4] and this was certainly true in my case. I had taken all the necessary steps to find forgiveness for my ex-spouse, but God knew my forgiveness could be even more complete. Something extraordinary happened seventeen years after that fateful day he walked out that I would never have previously believed was possible.

It happened on Monday of Holy Week. It was about 2 p.m. and I was doing a last check of my e-mail before I had to hop in the car and wait for my kids at the bus stop. A Facebook notification came in with the following message: "Hi, Lisa! Bob (my former husband . . . we'll call him Bob) wants to be friends on Facebook." And there, staring at me with a happy smile, was a picture of him with his wife and three children. His personal message read, "Lisa, I can't believe it's you! How have you been?"

I felt like I had been slapped across the face! Was this some kind of joke?

There had been nothing but silence between us after a bitter divorce and he wanted to be friends on Facebook? My first thought was, *Did you forget what happened seventeen years ago? If you did, I can certainly remind you.* My hands began to shake with rage as all the terrible memories of what had happened flooded back.

I believed I had forgiven Bob years before and had actually called him once so I could say those words to him and make it official. So it was absolutely stunning and scary to feel this level of rage return in an instant.

Later that evening when the children were asleep, my husband Jim and I discussed it all. He asked, "Do you think maybe he needs some closure or wants to say I'm sorry?"

That volcano of emotion erupted inside me once again. "NO! The man is incapable of saying he's sorry! You don't know what he did to me or how arrogantly he did it . . . how he ruined my life! He doesn't want to apologize. That's impossible."

"Okay," Jim replied, "but you might want to think about that."

My brother asked the same question the following day. "Look, Lisa, this guy is in his forties. He's middle-aged. My guess is that he is at a point where he wants to say he's sorry." Again, the emotions overwhelmed me.

"*No!* Has everyone forgotten what he did? How deliberately he did it? No, I don't believe he's capable of an apology." My brother suggested sending him a benign sort of reply, you know, something like, "Hi, Bob, I'm fine and it's good to know you're doing well." I followed his advice and within thirty minutes of sending my response, I got the surprise of a lifetime. Bob had messaged me again. He wrote:

> Hi Lisa,
>
> I am truly sorry for the past. I was not a good person then and a terrible husband. I came to realize that after truly accepting Christ into my life. And for the heartache I caused, I am sorry.

The note continued, explaining how God had been working in his life after battling many demons. I can't remember a time when I was that stunned and amazed. Even though I had forgiven him, apparently there was this final step I needed to take.

We continued the discussion for the next several days, and although it was productive, it was also extremely painful. I felt as if I was living a mini-version of my divorce all over again. God had given me the gift of Bob's apology and at the same time seemed to be saying to me, *Come suffer with me a little more. Pick up your cross and walk with me to Calvary.* I spent the next several days of this extraordinary Holy Week experience in prayer, contemplating Jesus' passion and death and uniting my suffering to his. I reflected on him carrying his Cross and falling under its weight, then each time getting back on his feet and forging ahead. I could hear him saying, "Father, forgive them . . ." as he hung on the Cross.

On Good Friday morning, I awoke and the familiar pain that had accompanied my first thoughts every morning that week was replaced with an incredible sense of peace. There was not a sore spot in my heart to be found. I went down to my computer and e-mailed Bob for the last time. I told him I was truly glad he had made contact and that I would keep him and his family in my prayers for a wonderful life. That Easter became the most incredibly joyful Easter I had ever experienced.

I share that with you specifically to illustrate how, with God, anything is possible, even if the forgiveness you seek seems completely impossible. Divorce is so unjust, so painful, and it might appear that finding a way to forgive your ex-spouse, or seek forgiveness from your ex-spouse, is out of the question. But God's grace will pave the way if you ask for his help. He will certainly shower you with all the graces and blessings you need to forgive if you open your heart to the opportunity for forgiveness.

To begin this process, here's a simple exercise. Take a piece of paper and write down the first names of all the people you've been romantically involved with. Then, look at each of them and take note of how you feel when you see their name. Any twinges of discomfort or feelings of resentment or jealousy? Does it feel like poking a sore spot or slamming a door closed? You may have a different way of describing the feeling, but if it is a negative reaction, you've got some work to do.

As you go through life, there is no question you've encountered your share of hurts and disappointments in relationships. Whether it's a family, business, friendship, or dating relationship, we are all sinners and we all bring our faults and imperfections to the table when we interconnect with other human beings. So, it stands to reason that things will sometimes go wrong. There are far too many people in this world who refuse to forgive those who have hurt them and at the end of their lives have hearts that are bitterly cold. They leave a wake of destruction and broken lives behind them. This is why it's so important to have a heart free from animosity, jealousy, and indignation before you try to love again. It makes the need to practice forgiveness imperative.

Think about it this way: when you don't forgive people for their offenses against you, your heart becomes like a little detention center where all the people who have hurt you are stuck, forced to remain in tiny cells. You are the guard. You take them out from time to time and punish them. You angrily tell them all the things you wish you had said at the moment they hurt you. Then you lock them up again until the next time you want to punish them. How in the world is it possible to have room in your heart for love if it is full of rage? Where is the room to love someone new if your heart is filled with animosity toward others? Not only does a heart like this have a greatly reduced capacity for love but also the effects of holding on to jealousies and resentment take their toll. The time and energy you spend staying mad is time and energy you can't ever get back.

The good news is you don't have to live like this. Freeing your heart of this baggage is entirely within your control. You can put an end to the bad feelings and be free again. This kind of work is the good stuff; this is exciting work! The more diligently you apply yourself in this matter, the greater effect it will have on every aspect of your life. The culmination of hard work pays off in big ways. Now, let's talk about how to detach from these negative feelings that are holding you back and start improving your level of attractiveness.

Key #3: Detachment

This aspect might seem very much like forgiveness, but there is an important distinction. Forgiveness is a *moral* decision, while detachment is more a *practical* decision to let go. It requires taking action. Many of the saints practiced detachment through having a preference of embracing only those things that were God's will and letting go of anything contrary to that. This made it easier to not be attached to money, possessions, or disordered passions.

Right now, you may be clinging to thoughts that are holding you back, such as the hope that your ex-spouse will one day regret how you have suffered, or that his or her new marriage will fail. Whatever it is you are holding tightly to, these emotional possessions are preventing you from having a healthy perspective on life and relationships. It is important for you to release your grip on them and let them go. Only you can make this decision, but it's worth it.

Think about the 1997 movie *Titanic*. In the last few minutes of the movie, the great boat has sunk and the protagonists, Jack and Rose, cling to a wooden headboard to keep them afloat. After some time, one of the lifeboats returns to the sea of dead bodies floating in the water, hoping to find survivors. Rose realizes they can be saved and tries to wake Jack, but gets no response. After several seconds trying to get him to respond, reality sets in. He's dead. Rose cries, giving up on her chance to be saved by the lifeboat, which, by now is floating away from her. Suddenly, she opens her eyes and rolls over with a renewed desire to survive. She says goodbye to Jack then pries his frozen hands from the headboard and releases him into the water. He slips slowly into the sea, never to be seen again.

That is detachment. It's the act of prying the dead, frozen fingers of your emotional baggage from your heart and allowing it to sink to the depths of ancient history, never to return. This is what you need to do with all the things that are keeping you tethered to the past and preventing you from being free and moving forward. Take these emotions, these memories, and these old hurts that keep you tied to someone else and make peace with them. Then, release them into the past and let them stay there.

Key #4: Gratitude

As you were going through your separation and divorce, it might have been difficult, even impossible, to be grateful for anything. Now that those situations have settled down, you can look at the concept of gratitude with clearer vision. Gratitude is important because it enables you to move forward to a new phase in life. Gratitude enables you to look back at what happened and say, *I have survived that pain and I am better for it*. Gratitude heals your heart and provides a multitude of reasons to wake up in the morning and get out of bed. It opens your eyes so you can recognize God's hand working in your life.

You can also find gratitude in recognizing the hidden blessings that may have come about as a result of your divorce. You may not like the idea of associating the word "blessing" with "divorce" and that is entirely understandable. But if you give this idea a chance, you might be surprised at what you find.

- What has been happening in your life as a result of your divorce that you can be grateful for?
- Have you come closer to Christ as a result of your divorce?
- Was an abusive spouse tearing the family apart, and have you experienced greater peace because of that person's departure? Has a relationship with a relative or friend become stronger because of their support? Has God brought new people into your life who have been sources of strength and consolation?

Gratitude reveals your inner strength, it builds virtue, and you receive many great graces and blessings. So why not give it a try?

Key #5: Action

This final step will be a natural one once you have taken the previous four. There comes a time when you just know you've got to take a step forward, that it's time to move. This is the perfect time to begin the annulment process if you have not already done so. If you are unfamiliar with the annulment process, I encourage you to check out the appendix at the end of this book, which lists resources to help you. You might also benefit from checking out my divorce support program and my book *Divorced. Catholic. Now What?* at LisaDuffy.com.

Why Being Available Makes You Attractive

All of this, of course, comes down to finding someone special with whom you can have a lasting relationship. Just as much as you would like that person to be ready for it, you want to be prepared as well. You would never want to fall in love with someone who could not commit to you, which is why it is so important to make sure you are completely free to commit to someone else, should all the right pieces fall into place.

An attractive person possesses certain traits or characteristics that are readily noticeable, even it's just in passing. One of those traits is confidence, the kind of confidence that makes a person light up a room when she walks in it. Confident people look you in the eyes when they speak to you. They smile a lot because they are happy. Confident people are friendly and easy to be with. When your heart is free from the constraints of the past and is not lugging around a ton of ugly baggage, you will experience this kind of happy confidence that will attract others to you.

I encourage you to take advantage of the *Five Keys to Healing*, going through the annulment process, and any of the other steps outlined in this chapter you feel would help you become 100 percent available. The wonderful changes you will experience aren't just to attract someone else; they are for you, first and foremost. Once you experience this incredible freedom and begin dating again, you will begin to encounter love and affection again. Then, we're really going to have something to talk about! That conversation is coming up!

Reflect on Christ's Love for You

I thirst.

Those words uttered by our Savior as he hung on the Cross dying were understood by those around him to mean he wanted liquid refreshment to quench his thirst, so they gave him a sponge dipped in sour wine to drink. But what he was really telling us is his thirst was for souls, our souls.

It was as if he did everything he could to show us the depths of his love for us . . . he was beaten, mocked, tortured, and abused, and as he hung on the Cross, bloody and slowly suffocating, those words seem to indicate that he felt it still wasn't enough. He wanted us to know without a doubt that it was our love he was thirsting for. He still thirsts for our love today.

If you have ever seen a picture of the Sacred Heart of Jesus, you will see him pointing to his heart from which flames are burning, representing his love for us. But, there are also thorns surrounding his heart, and those indicate souls who are indifferent to his love. Souls who know Jesus but forget about him, ignore him, or don't have time for him. This is what causes him the most pain and why he reaches out to us at every moment of our lives.

As you work on this part of your life and making sure you are *available* to love, why not make an honest assessment of how *available* you are to Jesus? Why not take this opportunity to boost your level of devotion to him?

It is so common these days that Catholics will line up for Communion but never think about going to confession. They leave Mass early or sometimes don't come at all. Yet, he has sacrificed everything for us, and he is always there longing for our attention. All it takes from us is a simple act of love . . . *I love you, Jesus. Thank you, Jesus.*

As you work on becoming completely available to love, take confidence in the fact that in making yourself available to Jesus, he will give you all the graces you need for your state in life. Every trial you encounter, he will be with you, helping you. He will be merciful to you and bless your endeavors. So make time for him and show him you love him through acts of love and charity for him and for others.

Quiz: "How Available Am I?"

Rate your degree of availability by answering these questions on a separate sheet of paper using this key:

1=Definitely 2=Sort of 3=Not at all

1. I believe I have truly forgiven my ex-spouse.
2. I believe I have made a lot of progress in healing from my divorce.
3. I understand the essence of "why not date?" as it relates to my personal situation.
4. I have been through the annulment process and have a decree of nullity.
5. I am able to pray for my ex-spouse with sincerity.
6. I am looking forward to a new relationship because I believe I have a lot of good things to offer.
7. I am willing to refrain from dating for a time in order to work on the things that will allow me to become truly available.
8. My heart has released all its prisoners and set them free.
9. I understand the need to practice detachment and know the areas of my life to which I should apply this practice.
10. I believe I have many things to be grateful to God for, and they outweigh the negatives in my life.

If you are able to answer "definitely" to each of these questions, then congratulations, you have done the work necessary to be completely available! If there are any to which you cannot respond in this manner, then you have just identified what areas you need to work on.

Questions for Reflection

1. Have I used dating as a means to relieve my pain in the past? If so, how do I feel after reading this chapter, and what changes do I think I should make?
2. What are my opinions about dating at this point? Do I agree with the *Why Dating Didn't Help Me* section or not? What are my thoughts on that section?
3. Are there areas of the *Five Keys to Healing* I need to work on? Which ones are they and what are the issues?
4. What are some practical steps I can take to begin improving in these areas?

Next Steps

- Write out a simple plan for how you will work on any areas on the quiz to which you were unable to respond positively, and take action!
- Contact your pastor or visit your local Catholic Metropolitan Tribunal website for more information about the annulment process, download necessary forms, make an appointment with your parish priest, and get the ball rolling.
- Make a list of the things you are grateful for, even those you may have received as a result of your divorce, and bring it to Mass with you so you can offer your Mass in thanksgiving for these blessings.

Chapter Three

Being Affectionate

People say if you have a healthy sense of humor you can get through anything that comes your way, especially the disasters. I agree . . . sometimes, you've just got to laugh. For example, after my divorce, I needed a second income to help me meet all my financial obligations. I scoured the employment sections of the local newspapers looking for something part-time, hoping to avoid waiting tables or working a graveyard shift.

I ended up accepting a position as a telemarketer, which offered evening hours and was conveniently located right around the corner from my house. But it was for a dating service. So, during the day I was fighting my way through a nasty, bitter divorce, and in the evening, I was cold-calling Los Angeles residents, trying to convince total strangers they needed to rush down and find the love of their life! Yes, a sense of humor can get you through just about anything.

But enduring the awkward irony at this job paid off, and I was eventually able to leave my day job and move into management. I transferred to a new location where I managed my own team of telemarketers. This was where I met Eric.

Eric was a very handsome and impressive co-worker, and I was thrilled when he asked me out on a dinner date. On that evening, he surprised me by preparing a gourmet meal for us at his house instead of taking me out to a restaurant. The dinner was fantastic and we had a lot of great conversation. After the dishes were cleared, we sat down on the couch in the living room and he began making strong advances. Before I knew what hit me, he was leading me toward the bedroom.

Freeze frame: Up to this point, I had been doing my best to live a chaste single life and my internal warning signals were blaring wildly. I knew if I took one step further down that hallway with Eric, I was going to be in big trouble. So instead of letting the situation get out of control, I decided I would turn the situation into something different.

Action: I stopped, turned around, and led him back to the living room where I grabbed a board game from his bookshelf, sat down on the floor with a pillow, and invited him to play the game with me. Eric hemmed and hawed and reluctantly gave in, but he softened up in no time. We played the game for a couple of hours until, finally, it was time for me to go home. As I left, he said to me, "That was the best first date I've ever had. Thanks."

You may be thinking, *why didn't you just sleep with him?* Especially after a divorce, adult men and women want to have sex because it's fun, it makes them feel desirable and attractive, and after all, they are already used to having sex with their spouse. So, what is the big deal?

There are many reasons why this is a big deal, but for me, it began with the fact I had always been raised to believe that sex was a complete surrender of myself to another and to have sex on a whim would be cheapening it . . . and me.

Sure, sexual intimacy might have made my date with Eric fantastic when we were in the moment, but I did not want to wake up with that "morning after" feeling. You know, when you had a great time but you can't really feel good about it because you knew it just wasn't right? I didn't want our date to end with that looming feeling of guilt.

The Joy of Sexless Dating

Plenty of people believe the Catholic perspective on having sex is too stringent, that Catholics are taught having sex is *bad,* and the Church frowns upon people who are doing it. But this is a huge misunderstanding. In fact, most people don't realize the Catholic Church's perspective is that *sex is a good thing and people should have more of it.* If more people enjoyed more of the intimacy that comes with good sex, the divorce rate in our country would drop dramatically. Because of the influence of the media, which tends to reduce the sex act to physical release, millions of people have missed the fact that there is so much more to sex. There is considerably more beauty and purpose than society gives credence to.

If they were to recognize the magnificent meaning of sexual intimacy and see the beautiful plan embedded in it, it would be easy to understand why it is reserved for marriage. People's lives would be dramatically different, and so many of our social problems would be resolved. In the pages ahead, we're going to explore this issue, but first, I want to point out something very important that was taking place on that date with Eric, a lesson I learned that has paid off over the years in so many ways.

That evening at Eric's house, something more was going on than just a testing of my willpower . . . I was actually learning how to be affectionate with a date in a way that didn't involve sex. Of course, I was happy the evening turned out so pleasantly—after all, when there is immense pressure to have sex, many dates don't end quite that well. But the true significance of that evening didn't occur to me until much later.

I came to realize there was a struggle taking place deep inside me: a subconscious fight to reclaim the virtues I had developed before they got lost in the devastation of my divorce and to redefine myself as a person and forge my new life without completely losing myself in what I refer to as the *culture of divorce*.

The culture of divorce is my way of referencing secular society's attitude toward people who are coming out of a failed marriage relationship and getting back into single life—it's quite similar to a carnival barker calling you to come and play the games and ride the rides. *Escape from your troubles and forget your cares! Anything goes now because you are free!*

I wrote this book because, at the time, there was no dating manual or a handbook I could refer to for guidance. And yet, in looking back at this period of struggles and challenges of this time of my life, I can see God at work in those teachable moments, the lessons learned even in some of the smallest things. It was necessary for me to learn how to show affection in a non-sexual way because it is an important form of communication between a man and a woman in a relationship. It is a way to build the romance and stoke the flames of love without any expectations of sexual intimacy.

That's not to say sex isn't important—just the opposite. In the context of marriage it is a vital part of the relationship! Let's take a moment to look at why Catholics believe sex is so important.

Called to Love

What does the human heart truly long for?

If you went out to a busy city street and began polling pedestrians on the answer to this question, I'm willing to bet the most popular answer you would receive would be *love*. We want love; we need love; and we were made for love. This goes all the way back to Adam in the Garden of Eden. God had provided him with everything he could ever want and would bring him happiness, but he was lonely. He didn't just desire a companion, he wanted someone he could love and cherish. God knew this so he created Eve as a *gift* for Adam. So, for a few minutes here, let's consider this subject in a slightly more philosophical light.

"And then, the man said, 'This at last is bone of my bones and flesh of my flesh; this one shall be called Woman, for out of Man this one was taken.' Therefore a man leaves his father and his mother and clings to his wife, and they become one flesh. And the man and his wife were both naked, and were not ashamed" (Gn 2:23). So, we see it that by its very nature, sex is intended to be a *gift*. This idea might sound like a good thing at first . . . giving a "gift" to someone you like or maybe have fallen in love with but haven't yet married. But if you take into consideration the fact that the gift of sex involves giving your body *totally*, this means it also includes your *fertility*. *Be fruitful and multiply*, God told Adam and Eve, and we know he intended for the two to become one flesh (Gn 1:28). But is it really possible to share that kind of openness and transparency with someone you barely know, and to be that vulnerable with someone to whom you are not fully committed? Should you risk offering every part of yourself, including your fertility, to someone who may or may not still be in your life a week or a month or a year from now?

Even if you are confident that you can handle the consequences if the relationship falls apart after being that open and vulnerable . . . are you both willing to commit yourselves to raising the children who are produced as a result of this intimacy? Most people who are dating aren't looking to have a baby; they want to enjoy the freedom of adulthood and discern whether their date is someone they want to be involved with on a long-term basis.

So, a dilemma is now presented. If sex between a man and a woman is a good thing, how can a man and a woman who are dating and not ready to marry each other enjoy the pleasure of sex but not be bound by a natural outcome of sex, bearing children? This is where contraception becomes a part of the picture . . . so a couple can enjoy sex but prevent a pregnancy, a seemingly harmless resolution to the "problem." But let's not forget—*sex is not supposed to be a problem.*

This is how a lover becomes a user, where the giving of the gift turns into taking an object and using it for self-gratification. Under these circumstances, a woman is not giving her body as a gift to the man; she is using his body for her own pleasure. The intended subject of someone's love instead becomes an object of desire. This is where the guilt comes from.

In the beginning, Adam and Eve saw in each other complete goodness, an image of God. They were unashamed to give themselves wholeheartedly to one another in love, and saw in one another someone whose total existence was complete love for them, a communion of persons whose love was so great it could generate a third person.

Not only did Adam and Eve give themselves completely to each other, but they also experienced complete joy with no sense of shame or guilt. This is not something I could have experienced on a first date with Eric or in any way at all until I was married. The bottom line: Because you have been previously married, you understand better than someone who has not been married how powerful love and intimacy are. The idea of dating and becoming sexually intimate with someone else sounds like it would be just what the doctor ordered for your lonely heart, but it's not—at least, not just yet.

♥

> Intimacy with chastity comes down to one simple word: "Honesty." Chastity refers to "integrity," which is all about being honest to what something is. A couple simply needs to ask themselves, "Is this particular gesture of affection speaking a lie or a truth about the reality of our relationship?" If a particular gesture of affection speaks the language of exclusive belonging, which is found only in marriage, but the couple is not exclusively bonded (married), then that particular gesture is speaking a dishonesty and dishonesty will always cause hurt.
>
> —Fr. Thomas J. Loya, STB, MA

♥

You can read more about this in Pope St. John Paul II's ingenious work, *Theology of the Body*. This amazing book is actually a collection of 129 lectures he gave between September 1979 and November 1984. The Holy Father began presenting these lectures almost immediately after he was elected pope because he knew that society was missing a major piece of the human sexuality puzzle. He recognized there needed to be a deeper anthropology, a deeper understanding of who the human person is.

In this book, St. John Paul II unpacks this mystery of human love and sexuality in a way that is both beautiful and succinct. God created Adam and Eve as a gift for each other, and through their masculinity and femininity they were able to express their gift to each other. The pope called this the *nuptial meaning of the body*.[5] This experience of total freedom and innocence in giving oneself to another can only be realized in marriage.

He especially wanted to provide a deeper understanding about the human person and re-read the truths of Pope Paul VI's groundbreaking encyclical *Humanae vitae,* which discussed the critical issue of contraception in the modern world. Although its message was met with mixed reactions, I experienced a real sense of joy in reading it because of the promise it holds out for those who yearn to experience this complete and total intimacy.

It's exciting to know that the desire for love is a yearning that was put in our hearts by God himself. It's not just an itch to be scratched or a need to be met. Love is our calling, our purpose in life. We have been created to love. Searching for someone we can love is what we are supposed to do, but ultimately, the love we are really seeking is God's love.

So when the Church reserves sexual intimacy for marriage, it's not just another rule or regulation designed to make you feel guilty about having a little fun. Reserving sexual intimacy for marriage means something important for you as a single person. It means *you* have the unique opportunity to take showing affection to an entirely new level in the dating world. Instead of being just like everyone else who is out there having casual sex and expecting you to follow suit, show your date how awesome it is to be shown real affection, the kind that says *I respect you. You are worth something to me. I will not treat you like an object.* This is how showing affection becomes an art form, and why those who are affectionate are naturally attractive to others.

> Man cannot live without love. He remains a being that is incomprehensible for himself, his life is senseless, if love is not revealed to him, if he does not encounter love, if

> he does not experience it and make it his own, if he does not intimately participate in it.
>
> —Pope John Paul II

The Language of Love

Some years ago a friend of mine, Mac, had gone through a fairly uneventful but terribly painful divorce. He was devastated by the fact that he could now only see his two boys twice a month for the weekend, and the loneliness he felt in going from being the head of a family to a single person living alone was overwhelming. But he told me how, even though the anger he felt over what happened to his marriage made it difficult for him to go to Mass, he went anyway—every week.

What motivated him to attend Mass, despite the pain he felt, was something incredibly meaningful to him: holding hands with the parishioners during the praying of the Our Father. Mac said it was the *only* physical contact he would have with anyone all week. This served as a powerful reminder that he was not alone, despite losing his wife and children, and that his brothers and sisters in Christ would always be his family.

It is true, love needs to be more than just interior knowledge: It must be demonstrated. So the question is how can you be single, have fun and date, and still live the virtue of chastity in thought, word, and deed, as a divorced person? The answer lies in discovering this art of being affectionate.

In his bestselling book *The Five Love Languages*, author Gary Chapman talks about the different ways people demonstrate love for their partner. He points out that not everyone responds to every language, and most prefer one over another. Some people feel loved when they receive gifts; others prefer words of affirmation. For some people an act of service is what really makes them feel loved. But the overwhelming discovery was that, not only does each person have their own love language, but also they are attracted to people who speak a different love language than their own. So as you date someone and begin to get to know him better, you can discover how to show him affection in a way that makes him feel even more attracted to you.

If the idea of being affectionate without sexual intimacy is appealing but not something that comes naturally to you, here are some suggestions that may help you cultivate ways to show others non-sexual affection.

For people in general:

- Smile more and make eye contact that reveals sincerity.
- Give side-by-side hugs.
- Be receptive to a friend's request and do your best to fulfill it.
- Anticipate a friend or family member's needs and plan accordingly.

For someone you are dating, all of the above, plus:

- Leave a love note in his wallet.
- Bring her flowers.
- Compliment him on something good he has done.
- Call just to say hello.
- Leave the gas tank full in the car and a pack of her favorite gum on the console.
- If you have a long-distance relationship, send a care package.
- Spend an hour in eucharistic adoration for her.
- Hold hands wherever you are.

- Surprise him with a picnic instead of opting for a restaurant.
- Compliment her hair style.
- Send a card for no particular reason.
- Speak well of her in front of family and friends.
- Speak well of his parents and show them respect.
- Make her favorite dish. Help clean up after the meal.
- Surprise him with tickets to the game.

You may have many ideas of your own on ways to show affection to others, and I encourage you to make your own list and start looking for ways to put this into practice. When you do, I believe others will remember you as someone who is thoughtful and kind, and you will probably see a lot of these people return affection to you as a result.

Is Celibacy a Realistic Lifestyle?

None of us are perfect. We are *called* to be perfect, meaning we need to be striving to do the right thing at every moment, but because of concupiscence, we sometimes fall. This is the human condition, the struggle we all go through, but what makes this struggle honorable and worthwhile is forging ahead and trying to be good out of love for God and those around us, not giving up and rationalizing our actions.

I made my share of mistakes in the wake of my divorce, and I understand how intense the pressure to have sex is. When I began dating again after my divorce, there was no way I was prepared for that level of pressure, and although most of the time I was successful in avoiding close encounters of the sexual kind, there were times when my resistance was low and I gave in to sexual temptation. Sometimes, knowing that I could temporarily alleviate the intense loneliness and feel needed by someone else was a powerful bargaining chip in my struggle with my conscience.

The really tough thing about this struggle for me was the lack of moral support: at this time in my life I was surrounded by friends and coworkers who saw nothing wrong with casual sex. They encouraged me to do it. Heck, they were practically getting down on their knees at night praying to God that I would do it! I had only my sincere desire to do what I knew was right. If only I had known then about John Paul II's incredible message. . . .

But there is something that will help you to be successful in trying to fight this good fight, and that is surrounding yourself with like-minded people. I recently spoke with a friend of mine, Shannon, who has been divorced for over a year and really struggles with her desire for intimacy. "I know I'm not alone in this; I know there are a lot of other divorced people struggling, too, but I don't know them. So being the only one at work and among my family and friends who is single is what makes me feel like I'm the only one in the world dealing with this. The divorced women I know from my kids' schools or from the gym are not on board with celibacy; they date to have sex, so they're not women I can talk to about this."

Celibacy is not society's way, and you can easily feel like the Lone Ranger in making this decision, so it is important to consider arranging your social life in a way that will be a support to you. Think about it. . . . What kind of people are you surrounding yourself with? Do you maintain relationships with people who will likely understand why you want to be chaste?

I went through this discernment process when I was single. I took note of any relationships in my life that might have been holding me back, and indeed there were many. At one point, I actually ended up quitting my job as a way to end a few of the unhealthy relationships I had, which was the right thing for me at the time. It made all the difference in my ability to remain chaste and gave me a much better sense of hope and optimism. Although quitting your job may not be the right move, I encourage you to consider the relationships you have and whether or not they are helping you live a good life.

Another important way to cultivate a heart that is free to love, and to be purely affectionate with those we date, is to be careful about what we feed our minds. Just as we need to surround ourselves with people who are going to encourage us to pursue virtue, we need to be on guard against anything that objectifies other people.

The Eyes Have It

In my small hometown, an electronic billboard near the grocery store flashes a dry cleaner's ad with the slogan "Drop your pants here." It's accompanied by a photograph of a man's legs with shirt tails barely covering his groin area and his pants down around his ankles. The focal point is not a man's face or the store providing the service; it is the body as an object to be enjoyed.

Every time I go by this flashing sign, I'm reminded of just how much as a society we devalue and disrespect the human person. Our culture is permeated with pornography and other sexually explicit material: on TV, in movies and popular music, and in *New York Times* bestsellers. It's everywhere. These days, it's difficult for the average person to remain pure-minded with all the sexual images, messages, and innuendos thrown in our faces at every turn. Like you, I have to guard my eyes and ears nearly every second of the day to avoid impure messages that attempt to infiltrate my mind when I'm just going about my daily business.

Why is this "custody of the eyes" such an important part of cultivating a truly attractive personality and healthy relationships? Each person has an intrinsic dignity and should be the subject of someone's love, not treated as an object; objectifying someone is a distortion of love, which only seeks self-gratification. The opposite of love is not hate. The opposite of 'to love' is 'to use'—using someone for your own gratification.

Have you ever "OD'd" on something you love? Have you ever played your favorite song incessantly because you just love it so much and can't get enough, only to find one day you are so sick of it you can't take hearing it even one more time? Ever had a hangover after drinking too much or felt so full after eating you couldn't move? All of these indicate a desire for something good but using it for your own pleasure to the point that you get sick of it and you just don't want it anymore.

This is what often happens when people use other people for their own gratification. The solution to these problems is seeking the good of the one you love, not using them for personal gratification. If we don't remain focused on our end, the means become the end. Eternal life in heaven with God is our natural end. Once we take God out of the picture, life only has meaning in entertainment, which means all we seek is our own pleasure. In order to be able to love someone else, you have to be in control of yourself, and self-mastery comes with practice. Only then can we truly "honor" another person.

Showing Honor in Affection

Honor is a virtue that is not practiced as widely as it used to be, but it plays a key role in helping you become more attractive through knowing how to show genuine affection. Romans 12:10 speaks of the delight two people will receive in honoring each other: "Love each other with genuine affection, and take delight in honoring each other." In a romantic relationship, this delight strengthens attraction. Unfortunately, the sexual revolution threw out the idea of honoring others, elevating self-love and gratifying ourselves by using and objectifying others as the path to happiness and "freedom." And what resulted from this line of thinking? As a society we are faced with a dramatic rise in sexually transmitted diseases, broken families, and a plethora of social problems.

It turns out that sex on demand doesn't really make people happy; rather, it actually whittles the multi-faceted beauty of true love and true freedom down to a flimsy, one-dimensional, selfish impulse. Being affectionate is not sexual at all but an act of devotion or endearment—something you do to show love.

This is precisely why being skillful in the art of showing affection to others makes you so appealing and exciting. This is your opportunity *par excellence* to really stand out among all the rest of the available single people out there who are searching for love. In mastering the art of showing affection, you reveal to others that not only do you have excellent self-control but you also make it a habit to put others first. You can become the shining example of real love that knocks people off their feet and makes them want to know you and be around you.

Taking Up a Lost Art

It seems that in the age of technology, we are constantly abandoning things that take hard work or at least some effort in exchange for adopting things that make life easier, even if it means losing something worthwhile or important in the process. For example, the future of libraries across the country is in question now that you can order books over the Internet and have them shipped directly to your door or download them onto a tablet to read instantly. Who wants to take the time to drive to a library and then spend more time having to browse through all those books when a simple click of a mouse is all you need? Libraries have always been beloved hallmarks of our society, and yet, they are becoming irrelevant because technology is making things easier for us.

Don't get me wrong; my point here is not to demonize technology. Technology is a tool that offers tremendous power, resources, and convenience to the person using it, no question. We all love our smartphones, ATMs, and ability to download content in an instant. And yet, with all that power and convenience comes the slowly creeping assumption that *everything* should be easy and instant. It's a gradual mindset that influences our thinking to the point that we begin categorizing the usefulness of people and things, even if we don't realize we are doing it.

Think about it for a moment. . . . When you click on a website link and you have to wait more than a couple of seconds for the page to change, don't you get just a little uptight? When it takes more than four minutes in the fast food drive-through, do you become impatient and start feeling the need to remind the staff that it's supposed to be "fast" food?

This expectation that everything should be geared toward our instant gratification keeps us focused on ourselves and what we can get out of something. And with that, we become *users* and *takers* instead of *lovers* and *givers*.

As a society, our approach to relationships is becoming less and less personal. We text instead of talk, e-mail instead of write a letter, Skype instead of visit. It's certainly more convenient, but the end result is often far less intimate or personal. Taking the time to call and have a conversation with your friend, talking, hearing her voice, sensing her mood—that is personal. This lack of authentic intimacy, unfortunately, has affected the dating scene as well. Sex has become the predominant form of showing affection, creating a "hook up" culture that diminishes us, creating users and takers instead of lovers and givers.

He texts, "Hookup at 8?" She texts, "K." They don't go out to dinner together or have a meaningful conversation that might bring them closer together, and they don't show any real affection to each other because that would require giving of themselves and that would defy the whole concept of a hookup—using each other for their own pleasure. They meet at his place, have sex, and go on their way. Everything about their encounter is focused on *taking*, on keeping things "easy" and "convenient." Consequently, the real beauty and meaning of the sexual act is completely lost. In the words of Christ speaking to the hard-hearted Pharisees in the Gospel of Matthew, "from the beginning it was not so" (Mt 19:8).

But there is something wildly attractive about a person who is truly affectionate, someone who is attentive to others and is concerned with making others know they are loved. And there's a secret about this that not enough people understand—the more you love and serve, the more others want to return love and serve you. It's true! Serving someone else makes them stop and really notice you. People appreciate you and want to serve you back, which brings us to this bottom line: An attractive person understands that the true meaning of love is service.

> Affection is responsible for nine-tenths of whatever solid and durable happiness there is in our lives.
>
> —C. S. Lewis

Reflect on Christ's Love for You

A friend of mine, Monica, attended a conference for divorced Catholics some years back, and because she lived locally, she went home each evening instead of staying at the hotel. On Sunday morning, the final day of the conference, she found herself in a predicament. She was starving and could eat breakfast before she left, but if she did so she would have to miss receiving the Eucharist because there would not be a whole hour to fast. Or, she could wait to find something after Mass at the convention center. As she debated what to do, Monica felt inspired by a thought that kept coming to her . . . an interior voice that said, *I Am all the food you need.* Relying on this inspiration, she decided to skip breakfast and not be late for Mass.

Two hours later when Mass was over and the crowd was shuffling to the next event, the priest who had celebrated Mass approached Monica and asked her to help him consume the eucharistic hosts that were left over from Communion, and there were many. What a great grace she received in being selected to consume the extra hosts, and it happened because she was in tune with the Holy Spirit—his inspirations and his desire for intimate union with her. *I Am all the food you need.* God gives us everything we need when we come to him in the sacrament of the Eucharist.

The Eucharist is the sign of Christ's love for us and his desire to be united to us. Just as a husband and wife consummate their marriage through the union of their bodies, Jesus consummates his relationship with us through giving himself to us in Holy Communion. This is an awesome truth to contemplate, especially if you are struggling with the desire for intimacy with another person. Not only is Jesus all the food we need but he can offer life-giving intimacy in a way that no sexual encounter can.

When a marriage ends, so does the intimacy between spouses. Not merely sexual intimacy, but that deep connection that spouses have with each other: being one heart, one mind and one soul, as well as one body. This loss of intimacy on so many levels can shake you to the core, leaving you with nothing but emptiness. But, you are not alone in suffering your loss. God is not only close to you during this time but also present within you—Father, Son, and Holy Spirit. Each time you receive Holy Communion, you are united with God, the Blessed Trinity, in the deepest and most personal way, and God resides in you.

This is divine intimacy, and no other type of intimacy can be more precious, more loving, more valuable. What a tremendous gift! I encourage you to receive Holy Communion as often as possible, especially as you work on becoming more affectionate. Christ offers the gift of himself to strengthen you for the long haul and give you the graces you need during this important time in your life.

Quiz: "Am I Affectionate?"

Answer these questions on a separate sheet of paper using this key:

1=Definitely 2=Sort of 3=Not at all

1. I understand the importance of showing affection in a non-sexual way.
2. I feel comfortable giving compliments to others.
3. I believe being a giver in a relationship means putting someone else's good before my own desires.
4. It's important to me to have sex at least once with someone I intend to marry.

5. I agree that casual sex is not okay, but sex with someone you love is fine.
6. I believe it is important for my date to know I respect him/her.
7. I believe the pope is not qualified to teach others about sex.
8. I believe I am capable of being in a chaste relationship.
9. I find Adam and Eve's story interesting enough, but it doesn't really apply in today's world.
10. I think giving our bodies as gifts is better than using each other for pleasure.
11. My date would appreciate my listening with genuine interest about his/her day.
12. I am comfortable going out of my way to make someone I'm dating happy.
13. I don't have a problem doing something for someone else as long as they return the favor.
14. People who are not afraid to openly do nice things for others are very attractive.

Numbers 4, 5, 7, 9, and 13 are questions that should be answered as "not at all." The rest should all be "definitely." Once again, these are indicators of the areas you need to work on to be affectionate in a way that increases your level of attractiveness. If your score is off the mark, don't get discouraged; work on improving in these areas and you will probably find they will start coming naturally to you.

Questions for Reflection

1. What's my "love language"? How do I most like to give and receive affection (compliments, gifts, touch, time, or acts of service)?

2. Have I recognized the importance of showing affection in past situations? If so, how did that play out?
3. What kind of changes can I make in the way I treat people to reflect this idea of showing affection?
4. What do I think about sexual intimacy outside of marriage?
5. How would I feel if someone I dated went out of their way to show me affection, but made it clear that sex was not an option?
6. What are some practical steps I can take to become a more affectionate person?

Next Steps

- Write out a simple plan for how you will work on any areas on the quiz to which you were unable to respond positively. Then take action!
- Make a list of ways you would feel comfortable showing affection to others.
- Make a list of people you know to whom you can begin practicing showing affection.

Chapter Four

Being a Communicator

A few years after my divorce, I moved to the East Coast where I began dating a guy named John. We hit it off well, and I knew things were beginning to get a little more serious when he asked me to go snow skiing for the day at a popular resort.

Being from Southern California, I was well acquainted with water-skiing and was pretty good at it, but I had no experience whatsoever skiing in the snow. Maybe it was that whole *valley girl* mentality at work in my brain, but I didn't mention this to John. I assumed this small detail was not important enough to highlight because I believed my water-skiing experience would easily transfer to the snowy slopes. In hindsight, I definitely should have said something.

In addition to not having any experience on the slopes, I had no snow gear to speak of. This made our date an expensive one right out of the gate, but John generously stopped at the snow gear shop and rented everything I needed from the snowsuit and ski gear to the all-day lift ticket. Two hundred and fifty dollars later, we got in line and boarded the lift.

Whoosh! We both jumped on at the same time, but for some bizarre reason I lost my balance on the seat and slipped off, crashing back down to the snow from about six feet up. I landed at the foot of the line of skiers waiting to board with the wind knocked out of me. Not exactly my finest moment.

John quickly hopped off and helped me out of the way of the oncoming lift chairs amid chuckles from observers. Luckily, we were both able to find our senses of humor. We laughed awkwardly as we carefully made our way to the back of the lift line to try again.

When we got safely back on the lift and I was able to take a look around me, I marveled at the incredible scenery. It was a dark, stormy sky against the mountain of pristine white snow and it was breathtaking! But, just as I thought my troubles were behind me, our lift chairs passed over a landing platform and I accidentally scraped my right ski pole against it, which caused it to bend at a 90-degree angle. My mouth hung open with surprised regret as I lifted it up to see what happened, but John smiled politely and said, "It's okay, don't worry about it." Not only would my skiing be handicapped now, but I knew he would have to pay for my faux pas and that put a slight damper on the mood.

We finally arrived at the top of the mountain and following my date's lead, I jumped off the lift chair, *intending* to land firmly on two feet and start enjoying those slopes of powdery skiing pleasure. But, the moment I touched down, I slipped and fell flat on my back. Nice touch.

"Here, let me help you up!" John said, but as he grabbed me and pulled me up to my feet, I slipped again and brought him crashing down with me. Now John was starting to look a little annoyed. Okay, very annoyed. A four-year-old whizzed past us with a condescending smirk.

Suddenly, like God's commanding voice from heaven, the lift operator announced over the loud speaker, "She can't ski; she can't ski! Bring her back to the lift." Every skier at the top of that mountain looked on in amusement as they watched John drag me by my arm across a shallow snow bank toward the platform. Yes, this was the *piece de resistance,* the crowning moment of my humbling experience. The only way to fix this was to send me back to the bottom of the mountain. On the lift.

But, then we realized we were up against another critical obstacle . . . how was I going to get back up onto the platform? John had to remove his skis and push me from behind up the hill of snow where I could grab the lift operator's hand and be hoisted up. I'm sure you can imagine the scene and I guarantee you it was not pretty. Then, for one of the rare times in the history of the resort, the operator paused the lift in our honor. John and I got back on for the ride down the mountain. With a sigh of resignation, John asked, "Ready for a drink?"

Although I can look back today and laugh at myself, that day with John was difficult. It would have turned out much better if I had just done one simple thing . . . be honest with him and set clear expectations with him, like that minor detail of my having no idea how to snow ski.

Transmitting Love

Is it true that being a more effective communicator makes you attractive? Yes, it is, if you know the secret to doing it well. What makes someone who communicates well more attractive than someone who doesn't has much less to do with having a command of their language, excellent diction, or even a broad vocabulary, although those things do help. People who understand the secrets of communicating well are attractive because they are *transmitters* . . . they know how to effectively transmit *love*. And isn't that what everyone is looking for anyway?

The hallmarks of people who communicate well and know how to transmit love to those around them are:

- They are honest and straightforward.
- They listen *and* hear the person with whom they are speaking.
- They take into consideration opposing views.
- They show respect to the person with whom they are speaking.
- They are proactive in finding solutions and are not set on trying to win an argument.

All these characteristics reveal how open your heart is to love, how you treat other people, your level of authenticity (being the same person in public as you are in private), etc. These traits shine through any exterior and reveal the goodness inside you, which is precisely what you want.

I witnessed this kind of attractiveness once at a concert in an outdoor amphitheater with numbered seating. A woman was waiting for her companion to join her and she decided to go to the refreshment stand while she waited. Moments later, two gentlemen took both her seats. When she came back and saw her seats were taken, she didn't get upset or lose her cool. She approached them, smiled, and held out her hand to shake. "Hi, I'm Julie." They both reciprocated with a smile and a handshake as she proceeded to talk to them about how excited she was for the show to begin. After a few moments of friendly conversation, she added, "I'm sorry if there was some confusion, but you're actually sitting in my seats." The men looked at their tickets and realized their mistake. They very politely excused themselves, apologized profusely, and thanked her for being so nice about the whole thing. Most people become indignant in that kind of situation, but she handled it with great grace.

This woman was a perfect example of the kind of attractiveness that comes from communicating well and transmitting love. By the end of this chapter, you will have the tools you need to help you eliminate any negative communication habits you may have picked up during your divorce process and become a master communicator, a communicator who transmits love.

The Accidental Right Hook

In all my years of coaching men and women who have been through a divorce, I have observed one standard theme that seemed to be present in nearly everyone's personal story: at a certain point in each marriage effective communication became nearly impossible, and was a significant source of the pain they felt in spite of all the other hurts that were taking place.

When a marriage begins to fail, communication is typically the first thing to break down. It becomes increasingly worse during a separation, and by the time the divorce process is complete, the devastation can be irreversible. Many painful words have been spoken and agonizing conversations have taken place, events that at one point in the marriage were situations that were completely unfathomable. This is an experience that, no doubt, you surely want to avoid having to go through again.

This is why it is so important to take an honest look at how you communicate with others and understand why improving that communication will make you more attractive. It is too easy to learn communication techniques based upon knee-jerk reactions to volatile situations, and quite often, just like the assimilation of low self-esteem after going through a divorce, these newly acquired practices are not detected and addressed before entering into a new relationship. Negative habits such as these are almost certain to poison a budding relationship.

So, now it is time to begin shifting your focus from the adverse forms of communication you may have adopted as a result of your divorce back to the positive communication style of someone who knows how to transmit love to others.

Some of the most common communication pitfalls that take root after having gone through a divorce are:

- Speaking in accusatory tones.
- Shutting down emotionally to avoid a blowout.
- Being incessantly defensive.
- Using foul or degrading language.
- Manipulating others.
- Playing the victim.
- Listening but not hearing.
- Refusing to accept blame when appropriate.
- Using hurtful sarcasm.
- Fleeing the scene when it becomes too intense.
- Total lack of communication.

Although none of these communication styles are good or effective, they do have one common thread: They arise from the natural protective instinct we all have. Each one of these behaviors is indicative of having been hurt, and of attempting to protect oneself from further hurt. But operating on a defensive level is not a great way to communicate with others, and is not a practice that will draw others closer to you.

Imagine meeting someone who is extremely handsome or pretty and you begin dating but when a conflict arises this person uses foul language when he gets angry. Or she insults you with degrading and crude names . . . *do you find any of that attractive*? Maybe, instead of showering you with ugly words, that person just walks out of the room when the conversation gets too hot . . . *how do you communicate then*?

Isn't this many times the way communication happens when two people are going through a divorce? The yelling, the accusations, the name-calling, the insults deliberately hurled in every direction . . . this communication style may not be a part of every divorce, but if it was a part of yours, these are practices you want to divest yourself of as soon as possible so you do not make the mistake of bringing them into a new relationship. Frankly, they are communication styles that should be completely eradicated from the way you speak to *anyone*.

The best way to root out these bad communication behaviors is to have a plan of action. First, you have to identify the particular behaviors you struggle with and then apply a practical way to overcome those habits. So, if you are struggling with being able to accept blame when something is truly your fault, you will want to find some concrete way to practice doing this.

To transmit love you must be honest, humble, and concerned about the good of others.

Another aspect of communication that can be potentially harmful to a new relationship is your body language. Believe it or not, over half of the messages we send when we speak are visual, so our body language should convey the love and respect an effective communicator transmits. You know how it feels when you are trying to speak to someone about something important to you and that person seems to be listening but is distracted and doing something else? We have all experienced that scenario. Unless that person is in a real rush to catch a plane or in some other type of situation that requires them to keep moving, this type of communication does not work. They say they are listening but their body language sends the message that they are just not interested enough in what you have to say to sit down and give you their full attention. This does nothing to help raise one's level of attractiveness. But the bottom line here is these things can easily change if we put some simple, but powerful, steps in place.

Set Expectations

When you try to change a habit, it is important to replace the action with a different action. Once you have identified the problem areas you would like to improve, my suggestion is to find one of the human virtues to work on that will counteract the negative communication skill with a positive one. For example, if you find yourself complaining or being pessimistic, work on cultivating thankfulness. If you tend to be very self-centered or focused on your own needs, practice generosity.

The *Catechism of the Catholic Church* teaches, "Human virtues are firm attitudes, stable dispositions, habitual perfections of intellect and will that govern our actions, order our passions, and guide our conduct according to reason and faith. They make possible ease, self-mastery, and joy in leading a morally good life. The virtuous man is he who freely practices the good" (CCC 1804).

Sometimes you may need to cultivate certain virtue "clusters" in order to develop particular communication skills. For example, let's say one of the things you would like to work on is improving your ability to set expectations with others. You might, then, take a look at some virtues like honesty, trustworthiness, reliability, and fairness and think of what you can do to strengthen these virtues in your everyday life.

When you become adept at setting expectations with other people, whether it is a workplace relationship, dating relationship, friend, or family member, everyone is happier because they know what the agenda is and are on the same page. I could have saved John, the guy who took me on the ski trip, *a lot* of money and frustration had I simply been more forthcoming with details and given him expectations about my ability to snow ski. He likely would have given me a ski lesson and, at the very least, would have thought twice before bringing me to the very top of the mountain expecting a fun couple's ski down to the bottom.

Setting expectations is always the right thing to do, especially in important matters. If you are trying to remain celibate until marriage and the person you are dating is not in agreement with that, this is useful information you both need to discuss; otherwise there could be trouble brewing. He thinks you are a tease, and she thinks you are only after one thing; he keeps dating you to see how far he can get, and she keeps giving you the benefit of the doubt. It all leads to a lot of frustration and dissatisfaction. On the contrary, if from the first date or second at the latest you both convey how you feel about sex before marriage, you can easily make a decision to either continue dating and work together on this aspect or part ways in a positive manner. No hurt feelings, no frustration, just a mature decision based on accurate information. And, *it's attractive*! People like knowing what to expect and they respect someone who is not afraid to be upfront about their feelings or opinion on things.

Three Destructive Communication Habits to Avoid

Here are some other communication habits to think about that are potentially dangerous to a relationship, and some suggested virtues to counteract them with:

Bad Habit #1: Flashback assumptions. A flashback assumption is like this: you believe that, because you were hurt in a specific way by your ex-spouse, you anticipate that anyone you have a new relationship with does or will do the same thing. Learning to trust again can be very difficult, but it's important to work on this if you want to have healthy relationships with other people.

As an example, early on in my second marriage, I assumed that my husband walked away from our arguments and disagreements cursing and calling me names under his breath. That is something my first husband always did, and I assumed that is what all men do. One day after thinking that for way too long, I talked to Jim about it. He was surprised and taken aback that I would ever think such a thing. *I don't do that! I love you!* was his response. It made me realize how unfair I was being to him, even if it was unintentional.

Flashback assumptions indicate a lack of trust. After a divorce, trust is not always the easiest thing to regain, but it is critical virtue to work on to have a healthy relationship. A few other virtues to consider working on that could help to eliminate this behavior are fairness, sincerity, and solidarity. These are just suggestions that may help you overcome any doubts or lack of ability to trust that might be lingering from your divorce.

Practically speaking, what is the best way to overcome flashback assumptions? The first and best suggestion is always to pray. Taking time to talk to God about the things that are troubling you and asking for strength, guidance, and grace to overcome them is so important in trying to change negative habits.

If you are having trouble figuring out whether the problem is a flashback or a case of repeating old relationship patterns, talk to a priest or spiritual advisor, or seek the advice of a close friend who knows you both. It may be that you are choosing people who are not trustworthy to date, and you need to break this pattern. If you start dating someone who is known to be less than honest with others or who gives you indications early on that signal the warning bells, your warning bells might be signaling a need to end this particular relationship.

Bad Habit #2: Using profanity or crude language. I know, I know, it seems like *everyone does it*. Yes, it is in all the movies and in most television shows. Swearing and profanity have become the *modus operandi* in the media. But you know what? *Not everyone does it*.

Maybe you are someone who lets a few words slip when you get really angry and then apologize for the lapse. Okay, no one is perfect—go to confession so you can get a better handle on your temper. But if you want to become a truly attractive person, you do need to start over and make eliminating profanity from your speech a priority.

Many people do not even think twice when using profanity, yet they become highly indignant when the same words are hurled in their direction. Using foul language when you are communicating with someone—especially when tensions are high—is not only insulting but also puts the one you are speaking with on the defensive. These are not characteristics of a productive conversation.

A marriage and family counselor once told me how utterly surprising it is to her when she counsels a couple for marital problems and all they do is swear at each other and call each other terrible names. *I can't even begin to imagine this couple in love on their wedding day because they are so vicious toward each other* was how she described it. It is impossible to transmit anything good, let alone love and respect, when swearing or using profane language. The words you speak have real meaning, and they reveal what is in your heart, so choose your words carefully.

People who do not use crude language are more attractive people because they hold themselves to a higher standard out of consideration for the other person's feelings. They express themselves without the use of vulgarity, and this indicates a level of respect, concern for the good of others, and a personal decency that extends to the people they meet.

But perhaps the ultimate reason to change this pattern if you do partake in it is because, as a Catholic, you receive Holy Communion—the body, blood, soul, and divinity of Jesus in the Eucharist. If Christ, who is perfect Love, is living within us, how can we let such ugliness come out? That's just a thought for your consideration. Some great virtues to work on if this is an issue you would like to change are purity, respectfulness, charity, and self-control.

Bad Habit #3: Listening but not hearing. How is it possible to say something to someone who is looking right at you yet doesn't hear a word you say? Sometimes people are so preoccupied with other things, they forget to really *listen.*

Can you think of a time when something like this happened to you?

> Jack: Honey, do you have time to make me a sandwich?
> Suzanne: Sure, what kind of sandwich would you like?
> Jack: How about turkey on toast with plain mustard and no cheese?
> Suzanne: You got it!

A few minutes later, his sandwich arrived. His *ham* sandwich . . . *with* cheese . . . and *grainy* mustard on untoasted bread . . . wait, *what*??

Scenarios such as this are just the tip of the iceberg when it comes to listening but not hearing. I was recently at a child's birthday party and observed the grownups chatting with each other. The first thing I noticed was none of what was being said was really an actual conversation; it was all just talking. Chatter. People were exchanging stories and no one was asking any questions or taking an interest in what the other was saying. They were just talking at each other about their kids or their careers or their recent experience at the hairdresser.

I didn't hear anyone ask something like, "So, how did that work out for you?" or, "Are you feeling better now?" Not even a compliment on the new hairdo! Everyone just yakked on and on about themselves and their accomplishments. Me, me, me. Try that in a serious relationship and see what happens. The conversation will dry up quickly.

If you want to improve your ability to really hear what someone is saying to you, a great way to do this is to follow the Golden Rule . . . treat others the way you want to be treated. Start pushing the mental pause button on your thought process when someone is speaking to you and give them a generous moment of your time. I know this is not always an easy thing to do, but if you put it into practice, one day it will become your habit and will seem like second nature.

I knew a woman whom I greatly admired specifically because I had seen her do this very thing on many occasions. She was a school administrator and everyone knew her. She would be heading to her office with urgency and someone would stop her to chat. Instead of acting impatiently or even politely declining to talk, she would turn and give that person a welcoming smile and her full attention. I got my wires crossed one time and showed up for a meeting with her on the wrong day, but regardless, she sat and chatted with me for ten minutes. I knew she had things to do, but she didn't hesitate to take time for me and show a genuine interest in what was going on in my life. It is that kind of treatment that not only shows people you are listening but also makes them feel important.

Really hearing someone also means it is important to put aside any preconceived ideas you have about the situation or what you believe is motivating the person you are talking to and give them a chance to say what they want to say. You might feel confident you know what they will say, but even so, give the other person the opportunity to express themselves. There is a good chance you don't know what they will say.

Having gone through a divorce, you probably now have a greater appreciation for the art of listening, not just for what may have gone wrong in your marriage but because, afterward, you needed someone to listen to you and hear about what happened to you. Having someone to really hear about your experience and feelings was crucial for your healing, so it makes sense that really listening to what people have to say is key to good communication and getting to know people better.

To improve this part of your communication style, you might consider cultivating the virtue of patience, and in those moments when it is difficult to pause and take time, remind yourself of Jesus' words: "Amen, I say to you, whatever you did for one of these least brothers of mine, you did for me" (Mt 25:40, NABRE).

Sharpen Your Skills

> I've always believed if you put in the work, the results will come.
>
> —Michael Jordan

There are many things you can do to begin improving your communication skills in a way that transmits love, and one of the best ways is in mastering the art of giving a compliment. A sincere compliment can make a huge difference in someone's level of interest in you. People like to complain about other people's little idiosyncrasies and irritating habits, but think about it . . . when was the last time you heard someone complain about receiving a compliment? A better question yet, when was the last time you gave someone a compliment?

Compliments go a long way with people because we tend to become so absorbed in our own worlds and forget about other people. We walk down the street without seeing the world around us, focused on our smartphones or distracted by the music in our earbuds. As a result, our opportunity to interact with others is diminished significantly.

On the other hand, taking a moment to interact with those around us with a sincere, thoughtful compliment greatly enhances our attractiveness to others. Why not test this idea with the people you encounter every day? Tell the janitor in the public restroom how clean everything looks, or compliment the mother with a newborn baby and two toddlers in tow on how well behaved her children are (as long as it's true). They will remember your simple kindness for a long time. How about complimenting one of your associates at work on his tie? I have found, ladies, that men like to hear they have a nice tie, and I always point out the good ones to those wearing them. The list of possibilities is endless, but you get my point . . . compliments make people feel good and it causes them to remember you.

The *act* of complimenting someone becomes an *art form* when you stop focusing on superficial things and begin focusing on the deeper aspects, the things that take a little more attention to see and detect. For instance, compliment someone on how well he handled a tough situation, or on how you've noticed she is always thinking of others. This communicates a person's value and importance as a human being. Don't we all want that kind of validation? We all want to feel loved.

The other part of this "art" is learning how to give sincere compliments without using them to manipulate others. Anyone can pay someone else a compliment with ulterior motives, buttering him up so she can use her clout at a later time when she wants something, but where is the goodness in that? Sincere compliments come about because you've taken the time to notice something good about another person and you affirm it. That will soften the heart of just about anyone.

The world would be such a better place if we all complimented the people in our lives a little more. This kind of thoughtful treatment of others has the power to open conversations and heal relationships. But moreover, compliments open doors with people we don't know. So next time you have the opportunity to give someone a sincere and well-deserved compliment, don't hold back. Go for it and see where it takes you!

Four Temperaments

Another great way to become an artful communicator is by understanding the four different temperaments—choleric, melancholic, phlegmatic, and sanguine—and the roles they play in affecting the way people communicate with each other. Temperaments are part of your makeup, given to you by God; each person has a natural combination of two out of the four temperament types, sometimes in balance but sometimes with one more dominant. Understanding our and others' default temperaments helps us to best speak the other's language.

There are several excellent books you can read to find out more about the four temperaments—a few are listed at the back of this book—but here is a brief synopsis of each one:

- *Choleric*—People who have a choleric temperament are typically self-sufficient, bold, and driven. They tend to have intense reactions, both positive and negative, to people and events. They are often entrepreneurs and leaders but do not seek the approval of others for their beliefs and actions; they base their conduct on their own convictions. People with this temperament are often headstrong and impatient; however, when something needs to get done, someone with a choleric temperament is usually the perfect person for the job.
- *Melancholic*—Someone with a melancholic temperament typically has extreme highs and lows the same way someone with a choleric temperament will have, but someone with a melancholic streak is likely steeped in perfectionism. They have high ideals and tend to be much more emotional than logical. Someone with a melancholic temperament tends to see life and events through a half-empty glass instead of one that is half-full because of his or her desire for perfection.
- *Sanguine*—People with a sanguine temperament love to love others and be loved. They often crave attention and acceptance, have a happy-go-lucky personality, and are not easily discouraged. People with a sanguine temperament often have many friends because of their ability to reach out to others and enjoy life in the moment. Sanguines will also react quickly to situations and people, but those reactions are often short-lived.
- *Phlegmatic*—Someone with a phlegmatic temperament does not easily get his or her feathers ruffled. It often

takes a lot for them to get upset, even when things are upsetting. They have a relaxed attitude and will avoid conflict at all costs. A phlegmatic can be mistaken at times for not being sensitive to a person or situation because he or she displays little to no emotion.

If you know the basics about your own temperament and the temperaments of the people you deal with on a daily basis, you increase your ability to communicate and be a transmitter of love because you have a better understanding of who they are and why they act or react the way they do. Let's look at a hypothetical example of how the four temperaments cause people to react differently to the same situation:

> A golf ball comes flying through the kitchen window of a home sitting on the edge of a golf course, and shattered glass flies everywhere. In reaction to this, a choleric will jump up in a panic and coordinate a cleanup effort. A melancholic will be anguished that his picture-perfect world has been shattered along with the window. A sanguine will make sure everyone is all right and point out how good it is that no one was hurt. And a phlegmatic will pick up the ball to see what brand the golfer was using.

If each one of these people in this scenario understand their temperaments and those of the ones they are with, the choleric will not get upset over the phlegmatic's lack of emotion over what has happened but will understand it just takes more than that to get the phlegmatic riled up. The sanguine will not be upset that the melancholic is not more appreciative of the fact no one was hurt; the sanguine will join the melancholic in cleaning up and punctuate it with a hug. Each of these individuals, in their own way, is communicating in a way that transmits love.

Some Quick Notes

Here are just a few more suggestions you can implement to begin improving your communication skills:

Discuss your desire to remain chaste with your dates. This point is critical if you want dating to be a pleasant time, because sex is an expected part of dating after divorce for most people. Be as upfront as possible and *as soon* as possible. Don't forget how important it is to set expectations!

Commit to chaste speech. You can do it, you can do it! Remember that, although it may feel good to say it, it isn't good for people on the receiving end of those words. Resolve to eliminate any questionable language from your speech. Walk away or change the subject when someone tells a crude joke. Let your speech reflect the goodness and beauty of life, not the depravity of humanity.

Let your body language complement your words. When you listen to people, make eye contact and give them your full attention. Let them know you are taking a sincere interest in what they have to say.

Don't send mixed messages. For example, if you say you want to save sex for marriage but you wear clothing that says "Hey, look at my sexy body!" then this would be a mixed message. Be consistent in thought, word, *and* deed.

Reflect on Christ's Love for You

When Jesus was in his public ministry, he had little time to himself. The crowds were following him from one end of the sea to the other; people were begging him to cure their sick and drive out demons, and work all kinds of miracles. He had the Pharisees giving him a hard time everywhere he went, and even the apostles—as much as they were his chosen ones—were rather needy individuals as well. But Jesus found his rest, consolation, and strength in communicating with his Father in prayer. He would find a hiding place and pray all night and in the morning he would be refreshed. He leaves this example for us.

As you go through this process of rebuilding and refining, it may feel a little overwhelming to have so much to work on. You may have many pressing responsibilities and concerns about your future. Don't forget to pray as Jesus did and find your rest and refreshment in God.

Scripture tells us that apart from Christ, we can do nothing, so it only makes sense that daily prayer is how we remain connected to him. So, if you are feeling overwhelmed, there are creative ways to fit prayer time into your busy schedule.

Why not begin this way . . . when you open your eyes in the morning, even before you get out of bed, say a brief prayer and thank God for the new day. Ask him for strength. At noon, say a Hail Mary, asking the Blessed Mother to show you the way. Then at night before you sleep, review your day, noting the good things you've achieved as well as the failures. Thank God again. You will find great comfort and renewed hope by practicing this simple, effective prayer routine.

> I am the vine; you are the branches. If a man remains in me and I in him, he will bear much fruit; apart from me you can do nothing.
>
> —John 15:5

Quiz: "Am I a Good Communicator?"

Here is a brief quiz that can help you identify your strengths and your weaknesses when it comes to communicating with others. I encourage you to take your time in doing this quiz and really put some thought into answering each question.

Rate your style of communication by answering these questions on a separate sheet of paper, using this key:

1=Definitely 2=Sort of 3=Not at all

1. When I talk to someone, I put myself in his or her shoes.
2. I tend to postpone or avoid discussing sensitive issues.
3. I am prone to swearing at the person I am arguing with.
4. I would rather be silent than fight with someone.
5. My ex-spouse used to curse at me under his breath, so I assume everyone does it.
6. I find it easy to see things from someone else's point of view.
7. When I think I know what someone is going to say, I finish the sentence.
8. I frequently find myself telling others what they want to hear.
9. I have difficulty putting my thoughts into words.
10. If I don't like what you're saying to me, I *will* walk out.
11. If I don't understand someone's explanation the first time around, I feel stupid asking for clarification.
12. I try to divert or end conversations that don't interest me.

13. I frequently interrupt someone to make certain my views are heard.
14. I will stop a speaker in mid-sentence if I disagree with a statement he or she has made.
15. Send me an e-mail and leave me alone.

So, how did you do? Questions 1 and 6 are the only questions whose best answer is a 1; all the rest should be answered with a 3. Remember these quizzes are less about an overall score and more about simply identifying the trouble spots in your communication style. No one is perfect, and suffice it to say we all can use some bolstering of our communication skills, but if you answered a 2 in certain places, or missed the mark on other questions with a 1 or a 3, you will want to take those indicators seriously and map out some concrete steps you can take to correct these issues.

Questions for Reflection

1. Based upon the self-test on communication, what are the five areas of my communication style I most need to work on to improve? What virtues would help me overcome these obstacles and help me communicate with others in a more vibrant way?
2. Do I tend to shy away from confrontational conversations? If so, why? Which virtues would help me communicate better in this area?
3. Does my body language complement the words I say? Why or why not?
4. Am I comfortable giving sincere compliments to others? Why or why not?
5. If there are any communication issues that were not mentioned in this chapter but were present up to this point, what are they and how would I overcome them?

Next Steps

- Practice, practice, practice!
- For the next ten people you encounter, think of something positive about them and work that into your conversation. Any ten people—your mother, a coworker, the lawn guy, and the friend you are having drinks with this evening.
- Be the one to bring up an uncomfortable topic to discuss, a point of disagreement with a friend or a date, and simply listen to their point of view. Ask questions that will help you explore and understand their thoughts and opinions on the issue.
- If choosing the right words when you are angry is difficult and you have become used to blurting out those knee-jerk reactions using profanity, try repeating a simple mantra when you are calm like *Lord, give me the grace to love,* or *Lord, help me to be more patient.*

Chapter Five

Being Faithful

Shortly after my divorce was final, I left my home in Southern California and moved to the East Coast to begin a new life. I was anxious to put the past behind me and start over. I wanted to find new places, new friends, and new experiences, but I was also struggling with a deep sense of discontentment that had sprung from my strained relationship with God. In my quest to begin anew, I had a genuine desire to figure out a way to restore my relationship with him. I never stopped going to Mass after my divorce, but suffice it to say every Sunday morning, my life became a living hell for one hour as I sat in the midst of happy families, loving couples, and seemingly judgmental parishioners who all unwittingly served as reminders of my failure and loss.

I was angry God had allowed my divorce to happen, and unfortunately I allowed this anger to begin consuming me. I had lost sight of the fact that my ex-spouse chose to divorce me out of his own free will and, instead, blamed God for not doing anything to stop him from leaving. This anger created an enormous breach in my relationship with him, and in a twisted sort of way, I was consumed with an inappropriate sense of entitlement . . . *I have always been your faithful follower, Lord; how could you let this happen to me*? As if being a practicing Catholic and faithful Christian would somehow protect me from shame and embarrassment, from the pain and suffering that accompanies the Cross. Oh, how woefully misinformed I was.

Christ did not promise us a life of leisure as his disciples; he stated we would have to pick up our cross if we were to follow him. I was having great difficulty doing this. Sitting there in church, I often felt like a little girl stomping her feet and having a tantrum in front of her father because she didn't get what she wanted. This was something I knew had to change because I didn't want to follow the parade of disgruntled, divorced Catholics who had thrown in the towel and given up on their faith altogether. I wanted to find my way back to that strong connection I had always had with God before the day my life came crashing down. Restoring my relationship with God became my top goal for the foreseeable future, and I knew in working toward this, I would need to keep Christ's words always fresh in my mind: "If anyone wishes to come after me, he must deny himself, and take up his cross and follow me" (Mt 16:24, NASB).

As I settled in to my new location, I knew the type of friend I kept would play a big role in my spiritual growth, so I began looking for friends who were Catholic to help me begin rebuilding my faith. I was surprised to find that I was surrounded by Catholics! It was amazing to realize I was actually embedded in a place where there were so many like-minded people. Well, at least that is what I assumed the situation to be.

Unfortunately, I soon came to find out that my assumed "Catholitopia" was not actually a reality. I happened to be lost in a sea of *cultural* Catholics, or Catholics "by default": Those born into Catholic families who really don't understand the teachings of the faith or try to take them seriously. My roommate was Catholic, my coworkers were Catholic, my friends were all Catholics . . . but no one ever practiced their faith. None of them attended Mass on Sundays. None of them read the Bible or any Catholic books. No one was interested in talking about being Catholic. Many of them were divorced, too, but had a very different take on the whole thing than I did.

I was congratulated on my divorce with a hearty slap on the back and for "getting rid of the bum." Everyone wanted to set me up with someone they knew who would be "perfect" for me. At first, their desire to match me with men to date was flattering and I got a little lost in it. But it didn't take long for me to see through the hype and recognize their mentality was rather paganistic. *Live it up, celebrate, and have as much sex as possible until you find a relationship that sticks.* This gradually helped me become distracted from my goal of restoring my relationship with God.

> Although the life of a person is in a land full of thorns and weeds, there is always a space in which the good seed can grow. You have to trust God.
>
> —Pope Francis's interview with Antonio Spadaro, S.J.
> September 30, 2013

I was desperately unhappy at this point in my life, and I knew I had to change something. I needed to have people around me whose influence was positive, moral, and healthy. After spending time in prayer and discernment, I decided to quit my job in order to disengage from some of these unhealthy relationships I was involved in. I was well aware of the unique position I was in because most people do not have the luxury of just quitting their job for a purpose such as this. But there was no doubt in my mind that I had to make this move. I was still emotionally quite weak and I was being dragged down rapidly. It was very difficult to make much progress in rejuvenating my faith when I had no support system so I quit my job and eventually moved out of the city altogether.

When I gave my two-week notice at work, it was a bit scary because of the huge risk. I was quitting gainful employment and had no options for other jobs lined up. But taking this leap of faith paved the way for God to work my circumstances for my good, just as Scripture states: "We know that in everything God works for good with those who love him who are called according to his purpose" (Rom 8:28). Within a week, I was hired at a Catholic publishing company. And this is where I met a group of happy, practicing Catholics who would come to be the support system I needed so badly.

These everyday people—primarily married men and women—practiced their faith in such a beautiful way; it was inspiring and exciting. They loved being Catholic, and that was a breath of fresh air for me. They weren't confused over moral issues and they were passionate about reaching out to those who were. The example they gave and their level of devotion played a huge role in my ability to restore my relationship with God. It made me a better Catholic all the way around. As a single person working with mostly married people, their relationships also gave me hope that I would eventually meet and marry someone who loved being Catholic as much as they did.

In Good Hands

Everyone needs a support system in his or her endeavors. When you pursue a college degree, you typically are surrounded by other students pursuing their own educational goals. The same holds true with vocational goals; you network with like-minded people to help yourself move ahead in your industry. Spiritual goals are no different. It is important to have friends who understand your desire to grow in your faith and can even be of help in doing so. It's practically impossible for the seeds of faith to grow in your heart when you are being *choked by thorns* (Mt 13:8). It is critical for you to surround yourself with people who support you and understand you. Otherwise, you will maintain a serious handicap in your endeavor to become a better Christian.

You may be thinking, *What makes having a strong, personal faith in any way necessary or important in preparing to date?* Let me share with you the reasons why being firm in your faith foundation is so important to dating. Possessing a strong, confident, personal faith helps you:

- Make better choices when it comes to dating and getting involved in a committed relationship,
- Avoid future heartache in bad relationships, and
- Puts you on track to elevating your level of attractiveness.

Being faithful translates to making better choices because you are more likely to choose a relationship with someone who is compatible with your beliefs and morals if you are strong in your faith. Your relationship will be considerably more harmonious if you are with someone who shares your values and beliefs.

This also helps you avoid possible heartache in the future because a couple's shared faith typically becomes the rock-solid foundation of their relationship. They understand each other better, and have the peace of mind that comes with knowing they are united in their beliefs.

Being strong in your faith also makes you more attractive for many reasons. In the Gospel of John, Jesus told his disciples people would recognize them as Christians by the love they showed others (Jn 13:35). People who love without hesitation get noticed and so will you if your natural inclination is to love others. But being firmly grounded in your faith also reveals certain strengths and virtues such as confidence (as opposed to arrogance), respect for life, hope, trust, perseverance, courage, and the list goes on. These are all extremely attractive traits that draw other people to you.

Equally Yoked In Relationships

Did you know if you placed two acoustic guitars side-by-side on guitar stands and strummed the strings of one guitar, the other guitar strings will resonate with the same frequency? They come alive in harmony. It is very much the same with the relationship between two people who hold the same beliefs. They experience a beautiful harmony because they are in tune with each other.

In his book *The Exceptional Seven Percent*, Dr. Gregory Popcak reinforces this idea. He writes about something he calls a "marital imperative," which he describes as "a deeply held mutually shared set of spiritual values, moral ideals and emotional goals."[6] As we have previously discussed, you may not be prepared at this moment to be thinking of marriage, but this is still an important aspect of dating as you rebuild your social life. Why? Because the people you choose to date now will have an influence on the person whom you will eventually choose as a partner later on, should you decide to pursue marriage. Not only that, if you begin entertaining the idea that you may be called to the religious life, dating someone who is a Catholic grounded in their faith will be someone who will understand the importance of your discernment process and will likely support you instead of trying to distract you.

The happiest couples, according to Dr. Popcak, have a mutual identity and the only way to achieve this type of singularity is through first having a strong sense of your own identity and having someone compatible with whom you can unite—which reinforces my advice that even in social dating, you should be looking for like-minded people to spend time with.

Wouldn't you agree you date with the intention of creating happy relationships? Even when you go out with a group of friends, it is not very likely you would choose people who make you feel uncomfortable or awkward; you choose people around whom you are comfortable and happy. So it is easy to see how Dr. Popcak's point of seeking harmony in relationships begins in even the most lighthearted forms of dating.

> Do not be bound together with unbelievers; for what partnership have righteousness and lawlessness, or what fellowship has light with darkness? Or what harmony has Christ with Belial, or what has a believer in common with an unbeliever? Or what agreement has the temple of God with idols?
>
> —2 Corinthians 6:14–16

The Perils of Being Unequally Yoked

When you commit to someone in any way, you become *yoked* to them. If you are an employee of a retail store or food chain franchise, for example, you are yoked to the owners and their company philosophies and are representative of them to customers. But, many people have quit their jobs due to disagreements with company policies or corporate philosophies. Somehow, the views of the company were in direct conflict with the employee's beliefs or perspective on life, and the great thing is, an employee can quit.

Marriage, of course, is different because, as we know all too well, we are not supposed to just quit. We've all seen the devastation that comes from a spouse who quits his or her marriage regardless of the reason. So it makes sense that in dating, you would select someone of the opposite sex whose values and philosophies about life and morality are at least somewhat close to yours, which can help you avoid serious relationship conflicts in the future.

I personally experienced this several years after my divorce, when I dated a great guy named Seth. We were attracted to each other and got along very well because we were compatible in many ways. We could laugh hysterically and enjoy many discussions about our shared interests and passions, but when it came to discussing deeper issues, we kind of just danced around them because our beliefs were very different. Although some of our perspectives on life and morality were compatible, a lot of the opinions I had about social behaviors, moral imperatives, and, of course, politics, were in direct conflict with his.

We dated each other off and on for about two years, and finally I had to ask myself if I would ever marry him. I imagined what that would be like on many occasions, especially family gatherings. I had no doubt that a good portion of our life together would be fun and interesting, but the things that really mattered to me were connected to my faith, so I knew we would never be able to hold the kind of meaningful conversation a husband and wife must have because our faiths were not compatible and he was not interested in my convictions. When problems would arise in the marriage, as they do in every marriage, we would not have a solid foundation of a shared faith to fall back on. Finally, for all these reasons, I had to call the relationship off, leading to yet more heartache on top of my divorce and other failed relationships.

What I learned here is simple, and might be something good for you to consider as well: Even though I was dating someone I was attracted to and got along with on many levels, my faith and moral beliefs were more important in the end. Our relationship might always have been positive and intact if we had remained friends. True, sometimes these things are not readily apparent until you date and discuss these issues but I knew these things early on and could have spared myself the pain of yet another breakup.

Another important issue to consider is whether or not a potential date who is divorced is willing to go through the annulment process and hopefully receive a decree of nullity. As I mentioned in chapter 2, those who have a civil divorce decree are still considered married by the Church unless and until it is otherwise determined by the annulment process. Maybe your potential date is already going through the annulment process or possibly was unaware that one was necessary to obtain for remarriage and is open to the process. However, if he or she is not interested in pursuing an annulment, this could pose a serious problem for you. I encourage you to discuss this issue up front. It may sound too harsh to some, but imagine how harsh it would be if you fell in love and he or she was not free to marry?

Of course, the goal is never to be insensitive when discussing this issue, nor is it advisable to make that person feel like an outcast because of an unwillingness to pursue an annulment. Having this discussion may help lead that person in the right direction, even if you decide not to date. But have the conversation and you can simply state that because of your personal beliefs, you cannot date someone who is divorced without a decree of nullity.

Having these integral conversations with the person you are dating is imperative for a happy, harmonious relationship, and if you start seeing someone who fits in every way except in this realm of faith and morality, I encourage you to step back and consider how the lack of compatibility in these areas will affect your relationship in the future.

Skin-Deep Faith

Some couples don't regard faith as an important factor in their lives at all, let alone a key component of their relationship with each other. There are couples who feel that faith plays some role, but they approach the whole issue of faith as if they are rooting for their favorite sports team . . . *Go, Catholics! Go, Baptists!* They buy into the popular but misguided mindset that *God doesn't care which church you go to as long as you show up*.

But when times get hard, a half-hearted interest in God is not something that will support you like a solid faith that is cherished and shared between spouses. It's got to mean more than that, especially in a marriage. Some couples are able to make having different faiths or differences in the same faith work, but it is typically not the norm. Conflict arises and there is an automatic fracture because of the disagreements in each one's beliefs. Many times one spouse suffers quietly the entire length of the marriage because the other spouse has mandated there will be no discussing religion in the house. Worse still, it often means one spouse ends up leaving their faith to make the other happy.

Take Ed and Regina, for example, a wonderful Catholic couple I knew for many years who struggled mightily with this issue of faith. They met in post-graduate school and were members of a tight circle of friends who regarded themselves as intellectuals. Both Ed and Regina had been raised to be practicing Catholics, but over the years their quest for knowledge, science, and psychology led them away from their Catholic faith in pursuit of more "lofty" philosophies. Through conversations with the members of the group and hearing their opinions about religion, they concluded that belief in God was simply an outdated notion people held onto to make themselves feel better about their lives.

Several years after they married and were both running their own practices, Regina and Ed were expecting their first child. Shortly after giving birth, she conceived again, and before they knew it, they had two bouncing babies in the house. The children grew up and began playing with the kids who lived across the street—Catholic kids. One day, her son Joey piped up at the table while Regina and the kids were eating lunch.

"Why don't we go to church?"

"We don't believe in God, Joey," Regina responded.

"I do! I believe in God! Why don't you believe in God, Mommy?"

"Because he doesn't exist, son."

"Yes, he does! I believe in God and I want to go to church!"

This demand from her child shook her to the core. God was never spoken of in their household, so where, she thought, was this coming from? It awakened a part of her that had been silenced for years and didn't want to go back into hibernation.

As the days went on, there was an ache festering in her heart. She sensed a longing for her faith she had never experienced before, but all she could do was stifle it and continue on, business as usual. After several days, Regina was experiencing a real crisis. She couldn't ignore the fact that she truly did believe in God, and more than that, she missed going to church. The painful truth was, however, she believed she would never be able to tell her husband about her change of heart for fear of angering him. She was not willing to turn her "happy" life upside down just because her child wanted to go to church.

But, within a few months, Regina was wrestling with full-blown depression. She was angry with herself for being seduced into believing God was a crutch for people who could not cope with their hardships, and she was upset with her husband for being so wrapped up in the intellectual community that he deliberately ignored God. But, ultimately, she was depressed because she believed Ed would leave her if she admitted the truth . . . that she *did* believe in God and longed to bring his presence into her family. And here was the dilemma in which so many people find themselves: She wanted her relationship with God back, but would she take this risk at the cost of losing her marriage?

Ed was not clueless. He could sense the tension and distance she put between them, but would not address it. He, too, pulled away and their relationship deteriorated. Regina began going to the local church when she took her lunch break, just lurking around in the shadows at first for fear of being spotted and recognized by someone she knew, and then having the courage to kneel down and pray. Day after day, she would come and pray, asking God to show her what to do.

One day as she was walking out of the church, Ed pulled in and parked. Terror struck her heart as she saw him get out and walk toward her with a shocked look on his face. How would she explain this to him?

"How did you know I would be here?" Ed was incredulous.

Regina was completely taken aback. "What do you mean?"

His eyes admitted his guilt, for he had not followed her to the church; he had come of his own accord. "I feel . . . lost

. . . I've been hurting so much. But I couldn't tell you. You've been so angry with me and I don't know why. I came here to find answers."

They embraced each other tightly and cried. Then, they walked into the church together and prayed. That night at dinner, there was a joy present that had never been there before, especially when they announced to the boys they would be going to church as a family that very next Sunday.

The Flip Side

But what if neither of these scenarios describes where you are right now? Maybe you are not the one who feels secure in what you believe and are looking for someone compatible . . . what if *you* are the one who is unsure of what you believe? If this is the case, you should not feel bad about it and I encourage you to remember you are not the only one who has questions and may be confused or frustrated.

There are many people out there who have important questions about their faith for which they don't have answers. Oftentimes, they haven't necessarily pursued finding the answers because they have no clue where to look for them. But it is very important that you do not resign yourself to being blissfully ignorant. Receiving answers to your questions about faith will be like turning on a light inside you—it will broaden your perspective in a rather surprising way. You will live a much fuller, vibrant life if your personal beliefs are well defined and your faith will deepen in a way that will support you in times of struggle.

That being said, the thought of searching for answers about your faith may seem to be an exhausting proposition because of all the disagreements there are between atheists and believers, world religions, and even the Christian faithful themselves. With all the talk shows, news shows, magazines, and public opinions out there, especially in the political landscape, who are we to believe? It can seem overwhelming trying to listen, learn, and decipher what the truth really is. But, what is important to remember is if you don't have your basic questions about life or the Catholic Church answered, you will never figure the rest out. And who wants to go through life being totally confused? God gave us an intellect and the ability to reason so we can discover the answers we are looking for. But God also gave us the Holy Spirit to guide, inspire, and enlighten us. Praying to God for wisdom and guidance during this time will lead you in the right direction and help you regain your sense of self-worth, especially if you had to downplay your spiritual life for the sake of a previous relationship.

Case in point, I grew up with Craig, a friend of mine who was raised Catholic like myself, but in his early adult years he gradually let go of practicing his faith. For a long while, he just professed to be a Christian who believed in God but not in organized religion. He adopted a sort of *live and let live* mentality toward people and their different beliefs; *you believe your way and I believe mine.*

Then he met Alicia, the girl of his dreams. Alicia was in "church hunting" mode when she and Craig met and fell in love. He decided he would support her in her search by attending the different services with her but stated he was not interested in more than that. So they considered many different religions as part of the journey to find a spiritual home until, one Sunday, it all changed for Craig. They were attending a non-denominational service that seemed to fit them well, until the pastor unleashed a barrage of anti-Catholic rhetoric during his sermon.

Craig was distressed and confused. How is it he grew up in the Catholic faith and never heard these shocking allegations before? Even though he couldn't prove this pastor was wrong in what he said, he knew there had to be more to the story. Surely his parents would not have raised him in a church that was considered to be so evil? That experience caused a lot of friction between him and Alicia, who accepted every word the pastor spoke to the congregation without hesitation. She couldn't understand why Craig would be so defensive and upset about these claims when he wasn't even interested in being Catholic. Suddenly, Craig's faith became very important to him, and he knew if he didn't find factual information to rebut the pastor's claims, he would either have to give in to Alicia and ignore his aching conscience or lose her altogether.

This is not a predicament anyone would want to be in but it happens all the time because so many Catholics out there do not know their faith and often do not take an interest in it until they face extreme challenges in life. Whether you have experienced a situation like that or not, there is a very easy way to make an assessment on where you stand in regard to the teachings of the Catholic Church and it all begins with going back to the basics.

♥

> Living a more faithful Catholic life today is a path designed not just for priests and nuns, nor just for deacons and monks, but for us, the ordinary people in the pews. We must be lay witnesses who live as authentic members of Christ's family, the Holy Catholic Church. By learning and sharing your Catholic faith, you can experience the greatest adventure of your life as you give yourself more completely, more passionately, to the will of God and the promptings of the Holy Spirit.
>
> Today many families in our world are wandering along aimlessly. So many couples are searching for God, looking for peace amid the noise, yet they just don't know how to escape the urban chaos. Few people really

> understand that nothing other than God will completely satisfy their search for true happiness.
>
> The surest path to being a more authentic Catholic witness today is by living God's will, trusting the Holy Spirit to guide you, using your God-given talents to their best potential, and serving those who struggle with faith. It all comes down to surrendering yourself to God and trusting he will provide you with everything you need. God longs to fulfill the desires of your heart and make your dreams come true.
>
> —Tom Peterson, founder and president,
> Catholics Come Home, Inc.

♥

Getting Back to the Basics

Whenever things become confusing, frustrating, or so difficult they just stop moving forward altogether, the best advice is always to go back to the basics. When questions arise about your faith that you do not have an answer to and you don't know where to turn for the answer, there is a great temptation to remain blissfully ignorant and just let the questions remain questions. Many people go down that road, and what they miss is the incredible opportunity to find the answers to the questions and rise to a new level of understanding and confidence in their faith. Wouldn't you rather know the answers to the questions that keep you wondering and confused? And if you are secure, then these can be good discussion points with your significant other when dating.

A great way to get back to the basics is to go right to the fundamental beliefs Catholics hold to be true and make your own faith assessment. You can easily find these beliefs stated in the Apostles' Creed, the Nicene Creed we say at

Mass, and in the renewal of baptismal vows we say when we attend a baptism. They are all mentioned in each prayer and are all the same. Try it for yourself.

- Do you believe there is one God who is the creator of heaven and earth?
- Do you believe that Jesus Christ is God's only Son and he is our Lord and Savior?
- Do you believe Jesus was conceived by the Holy Spirit and born of the Virgin Mary?
- Do you believe he suffered under Pontius Pilate, was crucified, died, and was buried?
- Do you believe he then descended to hell and, on the third day, rose from the dead?
- Do you believe he is seated at the right hand of the Father and will come again to judge the living and the dead?
- Do you believe in the Holy Spirit?
- Do you believe in the holy catholic Church, the communion of saints, the forgiveness of sins, the resurrection of the body, and life everlasting?

These are our beliefs as Catholics, and after reading through that list, you may discover you do not believe in each one of those things or that you may have questions about them. Maybe you have no problem with these fundamental beliefs but don't understand the Church's stance on abortion or contraception. Having questions is always good when it comes to our faith because they help us grow spiritually through our seeking and finding answers. Run with those questions and pray for guidance as you do. At the end of these chapters, I have provided you with some wonderfully rich resources available to help you get answers to your questions. But first, a word about being proactive, being your own advocate.

Be Your Own Advocate

The best way to begin resolving faith issues you may have is by tapping in to your support system and looking for help from within the circle of friends and family you trust. But what if you don't have a network of support? You don't have to tolerate situations that are detrimental to your emotional, spiritual, or physical well-being, even if it seems like there are no options. If you don't have that kind of flexibility and are lacking the network of support necessary to move forward in rebuilding your life in a healthy manner, you do not have to put up with the status quo; you can become your own advocate and take advantage of the many resources available to you to find the answers you seek.

What does becoming your own advocate look like? First, it means you *take some time to identify and honestly reflect on the areas of your life with which you are dissatisfied*, particularly in regard to the people with whom you have surrounded yourself. Are they like-minded? Do they understand why you feel strongly about the things that are important to you and support you in them? Are they encouraging you in the right direction? Once you've put some candid thought into these questions, put your answers down on a piece of paper and read it.

Next, *ask yourself what changes you would make if you could*, and write those answers down, too.

Then, *find a way to take action*. Being your own best advocate means speaking up for yourself and not just accepting things as status quo.

For example, if you find your spiritual growth is stunted and for whatever reason you do not have adults in your life who can lead you spiritually, don't sit back and feel you have no options. Talking to your parish priest is a great way to begin these important conversations. Check with your local parish to see if one of the priests would accept the role of being your spiritual director. If they are not able to, see if they would give you a recommendation for other parishioners who are spiritually advanced and may be in a position to give you some spiritual guidance.

Another great resource to check out is the *Catechism of the Catholic Church*. Available in book form as well as on online reference version, the *Catechism* can answer just about any question you might have, even the ones that are so tough they boggle your mind.

You can also find any retreats that might be happening in your area and attend one. Silent retreats, which are based upon the Spiritual Exercises of St. Ignatius, are a wonderful way to grow in your spirituality as well as meet other like-minded people. Some other options would be to attend parish functions or even look into any Catholic singles events that might be happening in your area. There is always MeetUp.com, a website where you can find groups of people who meet in groups and talk about their mutual interests, helping each other advance and offering support. These groups range from writing circles and book clubs to Christian moms groups, sporting groups, and just about any other hobby, pastime, or life passion you can think of. Becoming your own advocate could be the gutsiest move you make. And if you do, I am willing to bet you will be very happy you did.

Catholic Resources

If you need help in resolving issues, there are literally thousands of excellent places to find your answers and feel confident you are getting accurate information. At the end of this book, I have provided a list of resources you can access right away: outstanding books; websites that offer videos, podcasts, and articles; adult enrichment groups at parishes; etc. But if you are in need of an answer fast, there are also some great radio shows you can listen to, call in to, and receive reliable answers to questions about the faith.

So, for instance, if you believe the Church's stance on sex outside of marriage or contraception is outdated and unfair, call in to a radio show and voice your opinion, make an appointment with your priest, seek out a website, or pick up a book. The bottom line in being your own advocate is to simply act on your own behalf and get your questions answered. Don't wait for someone to reach out to you; reach out through all the means readily available at your disposal.

Your Best Bet: The Sacraments

The best advice anyone can give you if you are struggling with your faith is to receive the Sacraments frequently and spend time in eucharistic adoration as often as possible. There is nothing that can bring more grace, more wisdom, and more fulfillment than in receiving the Holy Eucharist and receiving the Sacrament of Reconciliation. The sacraments contain all we need to be fortified for the quest to know our faith; this realization inspired me to pen the following poem:

> Through the sacraments of my faith, I am reborn.
> God's grace enters my soul like a refreshing breeze
> that rustles the leaves of the trees in a spring garden.
>
> My soul awakens with new life and rejoices because,
> once again,
> I am with my Savior, the One who loves me.
> Together, we walk through the garden
> and talk about all that is important to me.

I pray, dear Lord, that you will always be pleased
to find your home in the garden of my soul.
May you always take delight in my love for you,
a love that blooms like the first rose of springtime.

Spending time in eucharistic adoration is also another fantastic way to know God and come closer to him. In case you are not familiar with the practice of eucharistic adoration, allow me to explain. Many parishes offer eucharistic adoration, which is when a consecrated host is placed in a monstrance, an open, transparent receptacle that displays the host for veneration. Being able to see Jesus, visibly present under the appearance of the small white host, provides an intimacy between God and all who come to adore him that is only second to receiving him in Holy Communion.

People usually spend one hour in adoration, referred to as a "Holy Hour," but stopping in for a few minutes and making a visit can be very beneficial, too. The time can be spent any way you want. You might begin by meditating silently and gazing on the sacred host. It is perfectly fine to silently speak to Jesus from your mind and heart. You can pray the Rosary, read the Bible, or just relax and enjoy the peace and consolation that comes from being in the presence of God.

So many people chase after happiness in a worldly manner, not realizing the fulfillment they seek is right in front of them when they go to church, Jesus in the Eucharist. It is easy to believe that fulfillment is defined by the quality and quantity of earthly possessions. Dream homes are often sought after by following a simple rule of thumb: "Location, location, location!" But, I propose a different rule of thumb to attain happiness . . . adoration, adoration, adoration!

Spending time in adoration of the Blessed Sacrament is the surest way to find healing from your hurts and troubles. The sacraments and a solid relationship with Christ will bring you true and complete happiness in this life and the next.

A Final Note

Consistently growing in faith, rather than remaining complacent, is an attractive quality to possess. As your faith grows so will your level of confidence, trust in God, peace of mind, and happy disposition. Devotion is also accompanied by the practice of virtue. Someone who is charitable, humble, and happy ranks at the top of the "attractive" list. So, if you're wishy-washy about your faith and have unresolved issues with the Church, *work it all out now* before you get into a relationship. All you have to do is some homework and pray for the Holy Spirit to guide you.

Reflect on Christ's Love for You

Seeking Jesus is something we all do, even the most helpless people. Take, for instance, the story of Bartimaeus, the son of Timaeus, whom we read about in the Gospel of Mark (Mk 10:46–52). Bartimaeus was a blind beggar who sat outside the walls of Jericho every day and was considered a nuisance to the population because of his incessant begging for food, money, and especially the attention of others. When Bartimaeus heard that Jesus was nearby, he called to him loudly and made quite a ruckus. The apostles ignored him, but Jesus told them to bring Bartimaeus to him. Jesus asked him, "What do you want me to do for you?" Bartimaeus wanted to see and Jesus gave him the gift of that miracle but only after Bartimaeus told him what he wanted.

What is it that you want? Have you had difficulty in your relationship with God because the pain of your divorce took over and separated you from him? If you do pray, what are you praying for? Do you trust that God wants you to be happy?

God wants you to come to him with all your cares, worries, concerns, hopes, dreams, and desires. It is not selfish to ask God for things that benefit you. He wants you to come and speak with him about these things. What is it that your heart most desires at this point in time? Spend some quiet time with God today and tell him what is in your heart.

> "Go," said Jesus, "your faith has healed you." Immediately he received his sight and followed Jesus along the road.
>
> —Mark 10:52

Quiz: "How Faith-Full Am I?"

Answer these questions on a separate sheet of paper using this key:

1=Definitely 2=Sort of 3=Not at all

1. God is important to me and I try to keep him as the center of my life.
2. I already know enough about my faith.
3. I enjoy being Catholic.
4. Conversations with friends and dates about faith and morality are a good thing.
5. I believe the deposits of faith professed in the Apostle's Creed.
6. I have a daily prayer routine.
7. I believe it is important to be equally yoked.
8. It is important to me that my date has a decree of nullity if he or she has been divorced.

9. Time spent in prayer is not as important as getting answers to my questions.
10. I pray for my future spouse and the people I date.

Questions 2 and 9 are the only ones you hopefully disagree with. As with the other tests, you now have a fair indication of what you need to work on in this area.

Questions for Reflection

1. What kind of network of support do you have around you? If necessary, what steps would you take to fortify this network in your favor?
2. At this point in time, how important is it to you to date or be in a relationship with someone who has the same beliefs and values you do? Is that likely to change in the future?
3. On a scale of 1 to 10, 10 being best, how would you rate your level of understanding your faith? Do you have any significant questions that need answering? If so, what are they?
4. What are your thoughts or ideas about becoming your own advocate?

Next Steps

- See if you have a friend or relative who could benefit from some spiritual growth and invite him or her to find the answers you seek together.
- Look into which parishes in your area may be offering eucharistic adoration and take some time to be with Jesus. You might even consider becoming a guardian (someone signed up to take a specific hour of adoration each week).

- Take advantage of listening to the radio shows listed about and maybe even calling in with your own questions.
- Take action on any of the items in the "Questions for Reflection" section and start growing in your faith.

Chapter Six

Being Magnanimous

I was recently enjoying a relaxing afternoon at the beach with my family when I had the pleasure of watching something wonderful taking place right in front of me. A stray Frisbee accidentally hit a young man taking a walk in the waves with his pregnant wife, and he playfully threw it back to the pack of rambunctious youngsters who were mischievously trying to get him to play with them. He pretended to ignore them and then dove into the shallow water to chase them, sending squeals and laughter from the children into the salty air. His wife looked on with a smile as he dragged them across the waves on their boogie boards and showed them a fun time.

After several minutes of entertaining them, he walked back to his wife and gave her a kiss, and they continued their walk. It was really a delight to see such a nice couple be so willing to give of themselves to these random kids and spread some of their happiness around. He could have easily declined and continued on with his wife. The wife could have easily objected to having her husband's attention diverted from her to some stranger's children. Yet they both happily indulged in making these kids laugh and have a good time. In my mind, that was a great example of this fifth attraction factor, being magnanimous.

Up to this point, we have discussed many aspects of what makes a person attractive, and hopefully, you have already begun to see a difference in yourself and the way others receive you. Now we are going to look at this wonderful virtue of magnanimity, a virtue that holds the potential to help you stand out from the crowd through revealing the generosity of your heart.

The word magnanimous comes from the Latin *magnanimus* and means great (*magnus*) spirit (*animus*). History has given us many famous men and women who possessed a spirit such as this, like William Wallace, St. Joan of Arc, George Washington, Blessed Teresa of Calcutta (Mother Teresa), and the many heroes of the September 11, 2001, attacks. These people, and others like them, are excellent examples of people who were courageous, generous, and high-minded in the face of great challenges.

It can be hard to go through a divorce and come out the other side feeling you possess a magnanimous spirit. Instead of feeling courageous or generous, you may be feeling rather beaten down and protective of yourself. Understood. But situations such as these are where the virtue of magnanimity is borne. It doesn't mean you are necessarily called to go out and conquer the world; it means you live it in your normal, everyday life circumstances. Pope Francis described the meaning of being magnanimous very nicely for us: "What does it mean to be magnanimous? It means to have a big heart, to have a great spirit; it means to have great ideals, the desire to do great things to respond to that which God asks of us, and exactly this doing of daily things well, all of the daily acts, obligations, encounters with people; doing everyday small things with a big heart open to God and to others. It is important, therefore, to tend to human formation aimed at magnanimity."[7]

For anyone whose heart has battled the discouragement of divorce, Pope Francis's words offer hopeful consolation: "doing everyday small things with a big heart open to God and to others."[8] Many of the great saints like Saint Thérèse of Lisieux, Blessed Teresa of Calcutta, and Saint André Bessette took this very path. Saint Thérèse never left the confines of her little convent after she became a nun, and she chose to live the smallest details with the greatest love, but did this in such a way that no one really noticed. Even when she died, the nun who was commissioned with writing her eulogy was at a complete loss as to what to say about her. Yet, today, Saint Thérèse is a Doctor of the Church. She is quoted as saying, "I want to spend my heaven doing good on earth."[9]

Blessed Teresa of Calcutta, the well-known care-giver of the poor and dying in Calcutta, India, and Saint André Bessette, a humble doorman from Montreal, Canada, both lived unglamorous lives in very much the same way, and like Saint Thérèse, are beloved and regarded because of their benevolence and great spirit of magnanimity. It proves that the tiny, moment-to-moment details tended to with great love are just as important and meaningful as the major achievements the whole world takes note of. If you thought about your everyday routine and all your responsibilities, you might immediately see opportunities there to practice magnanimity and commit these acts with greater love.

For example, each day you encounter many different people in various settings, all with their own set of problems and worries. It is interesting to take note of how many of the people you speak with will complain about their worries or have a pessimistic attitude toward life because they are consumed with themselves and their world. This is a typical scenario where you can not only respond to them with love but also influence them in a way that changes them.

For example, you could greet everyone with a smile despite the fact you are feeling stressed-out. You might make a concerted effort to make eye contact with everyone you speak to, and use the name on a stranger's nametag if he or she is wearing one. You could place your own cares aside, listen intently to another person's complaints, and offer some supportive words or even a little friendly motivation to keep persevering despite her or his troubles. In doing the everyday things with an open heart, people remember you for being positive, generous, and thoughtful of others.

Many years ago at a time when my family was experiencing financial difficulties, I was the recipient of someone else's magnanimity. I was at the checkout counter at the grocery store and caught in an embarrassing predicament . . . not enough money for the groceries I was trying to purchase. I was frantically searching my purse, praying I would discover the additional $4.67 I needed to pay for my groceries but knew I did not have. Customers in line behind me sighed and rolled their eyes and tapped their feet impatiently. The cashier glared at me like I was an idiot.

Well, I had kept everyone waiting long enough. I knew I had to admit I could not afford my groceries. I blinked away the tears, swallowed my emotions, and got on with it. "Okay, let's put that box of cereal back, and that box of graham crackers and I should be okay, then." I handed the cashier my two twenty-dollar bills—and now I was broke until payday.

Out of the blue, a woman in line stepped forward and handed me a ten-dollar bill. "Get what you need and keep the change," she said with a smile and a gentle rub on my shoulder. I was humiliated but extremely grateful, and I thanked her two or three times as I walked out of the store with my children. That simple act of kindness was the nicest thing anyone had done for me in a long time, and it gave me a little boost in my otherwise very stressed-out life. Not only that, I have no doubt she sent a great message to everyone standing there watching the incident; *it is good to care for others*.

Everyday Heroes and Saints

In chapter 1, we talked a lot about remembering your divorce was something that happened to you but it didn't *define* you. It was important to lay the foundation for the work you would be doing and the growth you would experience by emphasizing your dignity as a son or daughter of our heavenly Father and all the gifts and talents he has given you. The seed of magnanimity already lies in your heart even if you don't recognize it because of the interior distress of your divorce. Yet, it is there and ready to grow and flourish as you begin to nurture it. Yes, even divorce presents opportunities to practice the virtue of magnanimity.

My friends Mark and his wife, Tina, divorced after fourteen years of marriage and three children. Although their relationship had had its difficulties for a long time, Mark was still taken completely by surprise the day he came home and found his wife had packed up the kids and moved out. She hadn't said a word to him; she just left an empty house for him to find. They would never be a whole family again.

Shortly thereafter, Mark found himself embroiled in a nasty and very costly custody battle that left him financially bankrupt, and eventually, he had to close the doors on the successful small business he had owned for years. He also lost his house and even with his degree and experience had great difficulty finding a job.

Mark and I spoke often about what was happening with him and his children. It was beyond challenging to keep his head above water after all that had happened and try to still, somehow, be a dad in his children's lives. He was an emotional wreck, but despite his personal concerns, he moved heaven and earth to be present as a father for his kids in any way possible. This was a great example he was setting, of course, but I was absolutely stunned by something else he was doing.

One evening as we sat together and talked about his situation, he was lamenting the extreme antagonism he was receiving from his ex-wife. Just when I expected him to pour out his bitterness over this and all his devastating losses as anyone would expect, he told me among the goals he had in trying to rebuild his life, the one that was most important to him and the one he worked toward each day was to try to see Christ in his ex-wife. "If I can't love her up close, I'm going to love her from afar," he told me. And he literally had things he did on a daily basis to make this seemingly impossible task a reality. Even though they were divorced, he wanted to show his children what true love really was in the worst of circumstances.

"Don't get me wrong, this isn't easy!" Mark said. "But I'm trying."

What a miracle was taking place in Mark's life . . . a miracle no one else could see. In the midst of such suffering and loss, he exemplified the meaning of Christ's command to love our enemies and pray for those who hurt us (Mt 5:44). The world would call him stupid, but I call him heroic. He was an incredible example of personal strength and charity in the midst of suffering.

Is there a possibility that any of Mark's examples might be effective in your relationship with your ex-spouse? Sometimes, the hardest thing to do is be nice to someone who has hurt you so deeply. You may have forgiven that person, but the memory of the hurt lingers and influences the way you treat him. Here is another opportunity to cultivate this virtue of magnanimity and take the high road when it comes to dealing with your ex-spouse. No doubt, there are likely many ways you can adjust the way you handle conversations or meetings with your ex-spouse that will influence your relationship with him or her and help you become more magnanimous. As Pope Francis would say, have *a big heart open to God and others.*

This is a great point to keep in mind, that being magnanimous does not require you to be perfect, and it is rather difficult to practice at times, but it does reveal the goodness of your heart and your desire to seek the good of others. God will pour out his graces on you in abundance, and with God's grace you can overcome any obstacle in your way. In a world where retribution and retaliation are standard responses to bad situations and people are too absorbed in their electronic devices to look up and see the person next to them, practicing the small things with great love is all the more meaningful.

> It is the characteristic of the magnanimous man to ask no favor but to be ready to do kindness to others.
>
> —Aristotle

A Greater Purpose

We have already discussed the fact that heaven is our ultimate goal and how all the things we do here on earth should be directed at getting us there. If you are magnanimous not only will people notice you and find you attractive but also you potentially will have a great influence on their lives.

This is the greater purpose of being magnanimous. *Don't just get yourself to heaven; bring a bunch of people with you!*

It is very much the same with your romantic relationships . . . not only will the way you treat your date influence him or her but also together, your relationship influences those who observe you. Your date will want to go out with you again if you treat him or her with charity and respect, but have you ever thought about how you as a couple affect the waiter that serves you your dinner, or the elderly couple sitting on the bench watching you as you walk through the park? The level of magnanimity you cultivate and practice will reach far beyond the person you are with, so think about it . . . you could be doing something wonderful for people you don't even know just through setting this great example.

Intended for Greatness

We see the importance of making the finer details of everyday life count in big ways, but what if you *are* called to do something big and great like being a political leader, or making films that positively influence the world, or running into a burning tower to help evacuate the victims of a sudden tragedy? What if God is calling you to step out of your comfort zone and do something big? Do you feel you are capable of answering the call or would you still let that label of divorce get in your way?

In the Gospel of Matthew we find the parable of the talents and read about the servants who were given money to invest while their master was away. They were expected to render a great return for what they were given. Of course, this tells us God expects us to use the gifts and talents he has given us as wisely as possible, which means you cannot allow your divorce experience to convince you that you are not worthy or you cannot do great things. On the contrary, the gifts, talents, and virtues you already possess are precisely what will enable you to push past the circumstances of your divorce and move on to greater things. This way, at the end of your life, you will hear God say, *Well done, good and trustworthy servant; you have been trustworthy in a few things, I will put you in charge of many things; enter into the joy of your master* (Mt 24:21).

♥

"You've got the wrong guy!" That was my response when I was asked to consider guiding the formation of a nightly newscast for a global Catholic television network. I'm a recovering alcoholic with no college education, and on top of that, I'm divorced.

A few short months later, I'm in the nation's capital anchoring and managing a dynamic nightly newscast for a worldwide Catholic audience. How can that be? With God, all things are possible, even after a divorce.

There can be great sadness in divorce, but the joy of the Lord helps us rise above it all.

It saddens me to see so many Catholics who believe a divorce cuts them from the flock. My experience is just the opposite. It is in my brokenness that I recognize how much I need the sacraments and my parish family more than ever.

The annulment process helped me to see more clearly the purpose God has for my life and become willing to go where he sends me and do the work he has for me. When God calls, he equips! He promises to bring all things to good (even divorce) if we serve him and live according to his purpose. I am a living witness to that promise.

—Brian Patrick
Executive producer / anchor, EWTN News Nightly

♥

Reflect on Christ's Love for You

You're too big for that, now. As a mom, that is something I have to tell my kids frequently these days because they are growing up quickly, moving past their childhood phases into more mature years. I just had to say this the other day to my youngest child who wanted to play on the crowded indoor playground at a fast food restaurant. But she is not a little girl, anymore, and is now well past the age and height requirement to be carousing in a tiny room with a bunch of little kids. So, here is something she must leave behind, and she must focus more on activities that suit her maturity level.

You're too big for that, now. Those are not words anyone necessarily likes to hear, because it means we're leaving something behind . . . something we like or are attached to, something that costs us to let go of in some way. Yet it is something we all must do if we want to grow. We need to leave a particular phase of life behind and seek a new level of maturity. I think, as adults, we most succinctly hear that call to leave the past behind and look toward the future in the internal whisperings of the Holy Spirit, when he is telling us it is time to move forward. And for people who have been through a divorce, this call to leave the past behind can be a difficult one to follow.

But, by this time what has happened to you should be changing you in a good way. Your divorce experience should be helping you to make wiser choices, not worse ones. It should be helping you understand how important it is to seek God's will first, instead of seeking only pleasure in an attempt to deaden the pain—to realize how precious a gift it is to be able to say, "I have loved," and be able to pick up and move forward. And when it comes to your ex-spouse, your experience should be shaping you into a more compassionate person, someone who is not out for revenge. The time comes when the Holy Spirit whispers, *You're too big for that, now.*

Let's always keep two words at the forefront of our day-to-day existence: time and eternity. Time, because each moment of the day you spend looking backward, you waste. You will never get those moments back. You need to look forward because God still has many good things he wants to show you, things he wants you to experience that will make you happy. And eternity, because everything we do here on earth counts in eternity. Let's make everything count.

> Strength and dignity are her clothing, and she smiles at the future.
>
> —Proverbs 31:25

Quiz: "How Magnanimous Am I?"

Answer these questions on a separate sheet of paper using this key:

1=Definitely 2=Sort of 3=Not at all

1. The fear of failure stops me from acting on the good ideas I have or things I am interested in.
2. I am a creature of habit—I resist the changes that come my way.
3. I am comfortable stopping to help someone who looks lost or in need.
4. I know I have a purpose in life and am excited to take action.
5. I am comfortable making eye contact with people.

6. I donate time or money to charities every month.
7. I find it challenging yet invigorating to roll with the changes and see what lies ahead.
8. I believe it is important to help my friends and family, even if it takes a lot of my time.
9. Children should be taught about the importance of helping others.
10. I hope the people I help recognize I was good to them.
11. I don't like stories of the saints because it reminds me of what a shlub I am.
12. I feel like I am sort of wandering through life, that I am lacking direction.
13. My ultimate goal is heaven, and I want to take a bunch of people with me.
14. I am involved in activities that enrich my community.
15. I receive more than I give when I volunteer to help.
16. I do not think it is important to give money to a worthy cause.
17. Unless they are part of my family, helping the elderly isn't my responsibility.
18. If the person in front of me in the check-out line at a store was a few cents short, I would pay the difference.
19. I enjoy motivating others to do their best.
20. I think a little humility goes a long way in dealing with someone difficult.

Questions 1, 2, 10, 11, 12, 16, and 17 are the only ones that should receive the answer, "Not at all." All the others should receive a "Definitely." As usual, note the areas you need to work on and take note of the changes you notice in yourself as you do. Let the excitement begin!

Questions for Reflection

1. Do I harbor doubts or fears that prevent me from cultivating the virtue of magnanimity? If so, what are they and why are they holding me back?
2. Is there someone I know or have known who has been an example of magnanimity that I am able to follow? Who is / was that and what were the qualities about that person I admired?
3. What specifically am I able to do today to begin fostering the virtue of magnanimity in myself?
4. Are there specific people or relationships in my life that are standing in the way of my becoming more magnanimous? If so, what am I able to do to help change this?

Next Steps

- If you have the means and flexibility in your schedule, consider becoming a eucharistic guardian so you can spend time each week with Christ and receive the graces, blessings, and wisdom you need to become more magnanimous.
- Take some time to get to know Saint André Bessette, Blessed Teresa of Calcutta (Mother Teresa), Saint Thérèse of Lisieux, or any of your favorite saints you find motivating for you and who is a great example of being magnanimous.

Chapter Seven

The Complete Package

HONK! I was rudely jolted back to reality when the driver in the car behind me laid on her horn. *Sorry*! I said aloud through my tears and waved. I had been driving home alone from a party that afternoon, and as I waited for the light to turn green at the intersection where I was stopped, what took place next brought me to tears . . . happy tears. Allow me to explain . . .

It was now six years after my divorce, and I was a completely different person from who I was when my ex-spouse walked out. My experiences had changed me and shaped who I was, but the work I had done afterward was what really made the difference in who I had become. I had lived those years alone trying to claw my way out of that deep, dark emotional well I had plunged into, and the fight to find safe ground again paid off. I had forgiven those who had hurt me, rooted out those spiritual weeds and problem areas of my life, and had found gratitude for my blessings and a tangible joy and excitement over what was to come. I made it out of that deep well, I had brushed myself off, and now I was ready to meet Mr. Right!

My married Catholic friends were always playing the role of matchmaker, especially Travis. One day, Travis called me at work with a very excited and urgent tone to his voice. A good friend of his was coming into town, and he wanted me to meet him.

I was cautiously intrigued. I say cautiously, of course, because I had gone down this road of being fixed up with someone "perfect for me" before and well . . . I was still single. But Travis insisted I meet them for coffee because this guy's time was limited and he would only be there this one day.

"Can you tell me a little bit about him?"

"Let's leave it a surprise . . . I'm looking forward to being the one there when you meet your future spouse."

"My . . . future . . . spouse?"

"Hey I'm just kidding, of course, but you guys are perfect for each other! So, whaddaya say? Corner of Third and Main at five o'clock?"

"I don't know . . ."

"He's a great Catholic guy!! You guys even have the same sense of humor! You will love him!"

"Where does he live?"

"Ontario."

"Canada?"

"It's not that far. And you know what they say, *absence makes the heart grow fonder*, eh?"

"What brings him to the United States today?"

"He's house sitting for a month and he has to be in Ohio by the morning."

"That's generous of him to do that."

"Oh, yeah, he's great! Poor guy lost his house. He had to quit his other job because he's been pretty sick. You might end up having to take care of him for a little while, but he's a good guy and you guys are a match made in heaven!"

"I'm sorry, Travis."

"Okay, but you're saying no to the man of your dreams . . ."

"Enjoy your visit."

Because I knew Travis was a good man, I had no doubt his friend would be very nice, but I was looking for someone who was ready and able to be in a long-term relationship. It seemed to be an obstacle I kept running into . . . many of the guys I met were either not interested in a long-term relationship or they were interested but not ready for one. I found this discouraging but I kept going despite the frustration.

Several months later, I attended a black-tie Valentine's Day event in New York alone and with *great* enthusiasm because someone I really liked—*and* who had indicated the feeling was mutual—was going to be there. I had high hopes for the evening and made sure I looked my very best, but I nearly died of embarrassment when he showed up with a date! I left early that evening, and on the way home, I had an internal melt-down as I had yet another one of those little-girl-stomping-her-foot-at-her-father moments.

Really, God? What am I doing wrong? Is there something I should change? Do differently? I know you hear my prayers so obviously you haven't brought the right one into my life yet for some reason . . .

Why was this happening? I had all my ducks in a row and was trying to do everything right. Shouldn't there be *someone* out there for me? I knew I was on the right track, but I also knew something was missing and I couldn't put my finger on it. That was until the day at the intersection when I came face to face with the missing piece of the puzzle . . .

I was driving home from a party I had been at with all of my married Catholic friends. It was fun and I was glad to be invited, yet it still reminded me of all I had lost and all that was still missing in my life. I had felt called to be a wife and mother since I was a little girl and I just hated the thought of not being able to fulfill that purpose.

The light turned red and I came to a stop, the first car in line. In front of me, there was a family walking across the crosswalk: a mom pushing a stroller and a dad with an older child on his shoulders. I watched, happy for them, sad for me. I wondered when, if ever, I would be able to be in their shoes. And that's when it happened . . .

Everything got still. There was no noise from inside or outside the car; it was just very peaceful. And in the quiet, I heard a voice that was so gentle and loving that I recognized it immediately. The voice said, *Why won't you give me this part of your life*?

I knew God was asking me to trust him. He was asking me to give him the control and allow him to bring his plan for my life to fruition. It was the most gentle, yet direct voice I had ever heard and it moved me to tears. I knew, at that moment, I had found the missing piece to the puzzle; I needed to include God in my plans. I needed to step out of the way and let him work.

And God was quite serious about what he wanted to accomplish. A short while later, I met the man I am married to today, and despite all those doctors who told me I had no hope of conceiving a child, we now have three healthy, beautiful children without ever having to resort to any medical treatments. In fact, when I became pregnant with my first child, the obstetrician sat me down in her office and said, "You do realize this is a miracle, right? Someone with your medical history should not have been able to conceive." I knew that my daughter was a miracle, as were her two beautiful siblings that followed. What an amazing life God gave me, especially after going through the devastation of my divorce.

Even though I know you may not be certain you want to be married again, I share my personal experiences with you because I learned a very important lesson in all that . . . God has a plan for you, just as he did for me. It might look similar to my story, or it might look very different. But as we go through this chapter, please keep one thing in mind—God is poised and ready to help you move forward and do great things with your life. *Are you ready to give him control*?

The Complete Package

Congratulations on making it to this point! I know you have done a lot of work. Now it is time to put everything together to form the *complete package, the whole person*. Becoming the complete package means you are at the top of your game as far as being attractive is concerned. You stand out from the crowd in all the right ways. You've worked hard on making sure you are truly available; you understand how to be affectionate in the right ways; you know how to communicate effectively; and you understand the importance of being faithful and being magnanimous—now is the time to bring all these components together under one umbrella, which is your trust in God's plan for your life. Trusting God with your future is the crowning jewel of all your work.

Start by arranging your priorities. Here are two illustrations, the first being how a typical person will arrange their priorities in life:

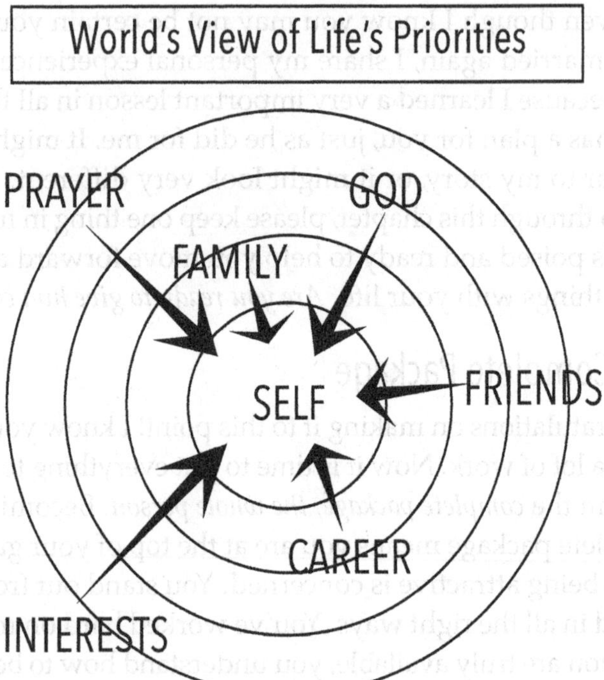

It makes sense to arrange your priorities around yourself because it is your life, but this scenario makes for a very self-centered life, one that focuses only on "what *I* need or want." Everything else comes second. The problem is this is precisely why so many people who have everything one could want in life still feel unfulfilled . . . their life is centered upon themselves. Since we all are imperfect human beings, there is no way we can find fulfillment based upon our imperfect selves. But, if we focus on God, who is perfect love focused on us, we find real fulfillment and peace.

Of course, you are the one who needs to live your life, but why do it alone? Why not invite God into it all and give him permission to help you make things happen? Take a look at the next image, which illustrates a better way to prioritize, with God as the center of your life and the rest arranged accordingly around him:

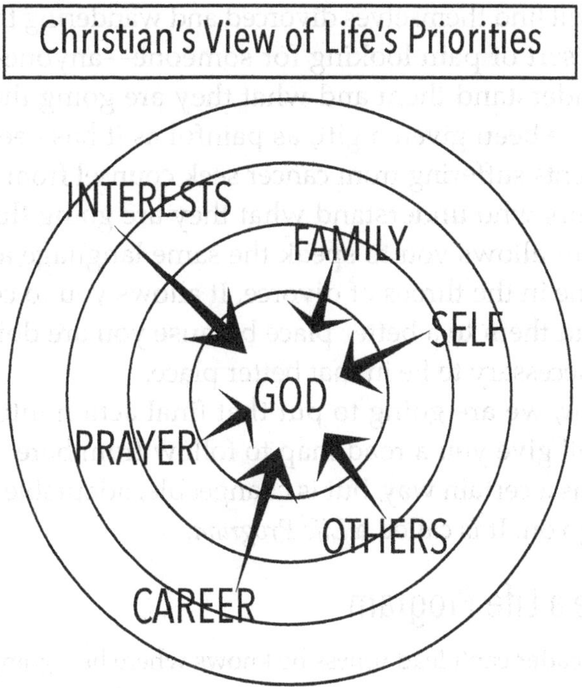

In making God the center of your life, you will experience a peace you cannot find anywhere else. Remember the words of St. Paul: "By the grace of God, I am who I am" (1 Cor 15:10).

You are able to do many things because God enables you to. He will give you the strength to achieve your goals and accomplish your necessary responsibilities. Most importantly, he will never give you a cross that is too heavy for you to bear. By arranging your life with God at the center, you naturally place your trust in him and will find a good confidence in all you do.

But it is more than this. The gifts you have been given and the lessons you have learned are given with a purpose—so you can lead others. There will, unfortunately, be many others who will experience divorce. People from all walks of life, all ages, and many different lengths of marriages.

They will find themselves divorced and wandering through that desert of pain looking for someone—anyone—who will understand them and what they are going through. You have been given a gift, as painful as it has been. Just as patients suffering from cancer seek counsel from cancer survivors who understand what they are going through, your gift allows you to speak the same language as does someone in the throes of divorce. It allows you to comfort and lead them to a better place because you are doing the work necessary to be in that better place.

Now, we are going to put that final action into place that will give you a road map to follow from here on out. It begins a certain way, but is changeable, adaptable, as the years go on. It is called a *Life Program*.

Create a Life Program

A leader can't lead unless he knows where he's going.

—John Locke, *Lost*

Once, when I was much younger, I was visiting a neighbor with my mother on a day when I was feeling somewhat depressed. I was rather absorbed in my thoughts and didn't participate much in the conversation they were having. I didn't think it was that noticeable, but apparently my silence spoke quite loudly. Our neighbor went into the kitchen to refill my mother's glass of iced tea and as she passed by me she touched my cheek and said, "Be happy!" She was obviously trying to cheer me up without being nosy or intruding in my personal business and I appreciated that, but as soon as I heard her words—*"be happy"*—my question was *how*? I wanted to be happy just as much as the next person, but I didn't see a path to happiness with the issues I was facing. It wasn't as if I needed therapy or anything, I just needed some guidance.

This can be a problem with many things in life. *Just do it* doesn't cut it. It is fine to have a goal or an ideal to reach for, but if no one shows you how to do it, having the goal can seem like the impossible dream. Dreams you cannot attain will not motivate you to take action.

So, with the help of a very wise priest, I took a few deliberate and concrete steps that would put me on the path to clearing the obstacles that were standing in the way of my being happy. I call it a "Life Program" and want to pass this incredibly effective five-step tool on to you and help you do the same. A Life Program is a plan of action that enables you to create a tangible and realistic guide—a road map of sorts—for becoming a happy person. It helps to tie together all that you've learned in this book and work on the areas of your life you need to improve. I want you to have something real to help you achieve meaningful personal and spiritual goals by removing the obstacles in your life that are holding you back from being a happier, more attractive person.

The best thing about creating a Life Program for yourself is, although the structure is the same for everyone, it is something you tailor specifically to yourself and your needs so it can be used by anyone in any situation and it will be unique to their situation.

Step One: Describe the "happy" you. Where do we begin? At the end, of course! If you are going to work toward happiness, you need to know what happiness looks like, right? So, you should begin by looking to the future and describing the *happy* you—who you are and what your life looks like when you reach your goal of being as happy as you can get.

Take a piece of paper, sit down, and reflect upon this scenario, and then as you look to the future, write down in a very detailed fashion how you see yourself if everything in your world were as right as it could be. For example:

- Describe what your financial scenario looks like.
- Are you in a happy dating or marriage relationship?
- If you have to work, what would your employment scenario look like?
- If you have children, describe what your relationship with them looks like.
- Describe your relationship with your ex-spouse.
- What about your spiritual life? What does that look like?

Although you should not limit yourself to these questions alone, they are a great primer to help you start determining what the happy version of yourself looks like. Here's an example:

- I own my own business, am my own boss, and love what I do!
- I have happily remarried in the Church and our relationship is doing well.
- We live near the beach.
- My ex-spouse and I have been able to learn to work together and have a peaceful relationship.
- I am on the neighborhood tennis team.
- I am a lector at church and feel at home in my parish.
- My spouse and I do almost everything together.

I highly recommend working on this first step, and all consecutive steps, while in eucharistic adoration. Whenever I have something important to write, I go there because I receive inspiration and guidance, so I highly recommend spending an hour with Jesus, asking for his assistance.

Step Two: Identify your obstacles to happiness. Everyone knows when you're taking a trip to an unknown place you need a road map to refer to in order to reach your destination. Well, that is exactly what we are doing in creating a Life Program, particularly with these next two steps. Now that you have defined who you are when your world is as perfect as it can get, you need to create a *road map* that will give you a realistic and effective plan to reach that happiness.

First, mark your "home base" or your starting point. To do this, make a list of the *five biggest obstacles* holding you back from achieving the happy life you have already described. At this point, you may want to use the five attraction factors we have discussed as a guide, or maybe you already have other obstacles in mind that are holding you back. Whichever you decide, the key to success at this point will be to identify the things in your life that are within your control. "Being divorced" is not something you can necessarily change unless you reconcile with your spouse so, although it is something you might want to change, it is a problem that needs to be broken down into smaller parts.

"I am angry about my divorce and feel depressed" would be an example of a better way to address this because it is something you have the power to change and it depends on you.

"I am still fighting with my ex-spouse even though we should be past this point" is another example of something you have control over. Take time to really reflect on these things that are causing you to be unhappy and write them down.

Now you may find that by the end of this exercise, you have made a list that consumes an entire sheet of paper. No worries, it is good to identify problem areas, but for your Life Program, you need to pick the five most immediate obstacles keeping you from being happy that you want to work on. Narrow the list down to the five points you feel are most important to address; otherwise you will be overwhelmed and risk becoming discouraged. Simplicity is the key.

Here is an example of what your list might look like:

Obstacles to Happiness:

1. I fight with my ex-spouse and I feel terrible afterward.

2. My child is angry with me and won't talk to me.

3. I have a deep resentment toward one of my coworkers.

3. I want to have a better relationship with God, but I don't really practice my faith.

4. I've dated, but I know I am not ready for a relationship yet and I find that depressing.

These are all hypothetical scenarios, but they are realistic examples of things that will certainly get in the way of a person being a happy individual.

Issues like these are quite often swept under the rug and never really identified or dealt with. They just become heavy burdens to bear, and many people do not know how to deal with them or get past them. Some people do not even realize they are carrying such terrible weight until they actually sit down and analyze themselves. That's one reason why creating a Life Program for yourself is so important. I encourage you to take time to make your list thoughtfully, again, while in adoration of the Blessed Sacrament if at all possible. When you are satisfied with what you got from this step, it's time to move forward.

Step Three: Figure out how to overcome the obstacles. The next step is simple yet thought provoking: Write down five practical ways you can overcome these obstacles. If you are using the five attraction factors as a guide, you may want to review some of your answers from the self-quizzes to indicate what needs to change and go from there. If you are addressing other issues not related to the attraction factors, here are a few suggestions.

For example, if one of the items on your list is to have a better relationship with God, then you want to choose one practical way to move you toward your goal of being closer to God. You might choose to commit to going to Mass every Sunday if you are not doing so now, or maybe Mass during the week if you are already a faithful Sunday attendee. You might choose to go to confession if it's been longer than a year since you last went, or maybe to begin going every month instead of just *whenever*. You might choose to commit to getting up just fifteen minutes earlier than normal to have some quiet conversation with God . . . spending time in prayer before you get ready for the day. Really, the possibilities are endless, but should be determined by you because you know yourself and your life.

As you make this list of five practical ways to overcome the obstacles you've identified, *make sure the means you choose are realistic and doable*. You don't want to set yourself up for discouragement by trying to accomplish something that is unrealistic or out of your control. Once you've got these tools in place, your road map is ready! And now, for the fourth step . . .

Step Four: What is your motto? Setting goals and priorities as you've been doing is a great first step. Now you're ready for the next step: Create a personal motto for yourself.

Having a motto is simply adopting a brief statement that incorporates your goals into words and reminds you of why you are fighting this good fight. It should be easy to remember.

Think different (Apple).
A diamond is forever (DeBeers).
Just do it (Nike).

These are all slogans that are memorable and focus directly on the product being sold. You can do the same thing for yourself as you work toward being happy by adopting some statement that will focus you on what you are trying to accomplish. For instance, if anger is an issue for you or you want to work on learning to forgive, a good motto would be: *Make me a channel of your peace,* from the peace prayer of St. Francis. This way, when you feel the anger taking over you can simply repeat your motto to yourself as a reminder of your goal. *Make me a channel of your peace, Lord, make me a channel of your peace . . .* You will find this is a tremendous help in getting yourself back on track.

Mottos come in handy most when you find yourself overwhelmed or experiencing strong emotions because saying your motto out loud or under your breath as a quiet prayer will remind you of your goal to be a better person, find peace in the midst of the situation, and move closer to being that happy person you've already described for yourself.

Step Five: Remember the saints are on your side. So often we ask others to pray for us and rely on their petitions to God on our behalf. This is the great thing about being a part of a faith community. But did you know that as you work and struggle to move past your divorce and on to a happier life, all of heaven is waiting for you to ask them for help as well?

The communion of saints—the blessed who have gone before us to heaven—can pray for you; all you need to do is ask them for their help. When you become overwhelmed, pray and seek help from the saints; they are one of the greatest spiritual resources you have.

Choose a saint to pray to and enlist his or her help from above. It's easy to forget that they have already suffered through this life and have gone through many if not all of the same struggles you are dealing with. Now they are happy in heaven, and their desire is to help us get through our suffering and be closer to God.

There are thousands of saints to choose from, too. Some of my favorites are St. Jane de Chantal, who for years was a single mother and had to learn how to manage the estate while raising her children; St. Padre Pio, who had a great zeal for souls and prayed diligently for souls and won great graces from God for them; St. Maxmillian Kolbe, who gave his life in a Nazi concentration camp for a family man who was being sent to the showers; and as mentioned previously, St. André Bessette, a tiny Canadian man who was deemed too weak to be allowed into the seminary and become a priest, yet through his humble service as a doorman at the seminary he was able to have built one of the greatest churches in the world, St. Joseph's Oratory in Montreal.

Many mothers can relate to the Blessed Mother, Mary. She is the most powerful intercessor you have. Many fathers can relate to St. Joseph. His prayers are particularly powerful for fathers and families as he was the head of the Holy Family. I encourage you to go online and search for prayers to these and other saints. There are many great prayers, litanies, and memorares to pray. Here are a few great places to find out more about saints: Saints.SQPN.com and Catholic .org.

Step Six: Look at your program every day. I keep mine in my prayer book so when I open it up in the morning, I have to see it. And I don't focus on the obstacles, per se; I focus mainly on my action items, the practical things I said I would do that would help me overcome those obstacles.

Step Seven: Evaluate your plan each year; let it change and grow with you. After a year of working on your plan, review it, see how much progress you've made, and then adjust it to fit the new you. You will be amazed at how much progress you can make in just a few months.

I've had a life program for many years now, and it has always helped me to move forward with achievable goals. So if you want to make the most of this great time in your life, get serious about using your life program and watch what happens . . . you will be amazed!

Reflect on Christ's Love for You

What would you think if you took your infant child to church to be baptized and the priest gave you a prophetic warning that you would suffer so much in life that "a sword will pierce your very soul?"

That would be pretty intense to say the least. This is exactly what happened to our Blessed Mother when she and St. Joseph presented baby Jesus to the high priest, Simeon, in the temple (see Luke 2:35). In contemplating this mystery of the Rosary and putting yourself in her shoes, it might seem reasonable to go forth from that point with an extreme sense of caution . . . not trusting, thinking twice or even three times before making decisions, and trying to remain in control of every aspect of life so as to reduce the likelihood of something bad happening . . . Yes, this would make sense to any parent.

But sacred tradition and the scriptures give us a very different description of the kind of parent Mary was, all the way to the end when the sword did, indeed, pierce her heart. She was kind, loving, and patient; humble, thoughtful, and generous. But probably her most astute display of virtue was her unwavering trust in God and obedience to his will despite her suffering. Everything she did was in accordance with his divine plan, even when she had good reason to fear the future or be skeptical. Her life, and that of those whom she loved, lay completely in the hands of God. This total donation of herself and her will was what enabled Mary to live a life of complete freedom and joy, despite the sorrows she endured. She was truly a beacon of hope to all that knew her and still is to us today.

Your divorce may have you believing that you cannot trust anymore . . . that God has somehow left you to fend for yourself. If you are feeling this way, I encourage you to contemplate Mary's example for us. Since the world is imperfect, place your trust and hope in the only thing that is perfect, her Son. Ask your mother in heaven to obtain for you the graces she knows you need to live with generosity, charity, humility, and joy. Ask her to help you live today instead of waiting to live when everything becomes just right.

> And Simeon blessed them and said to Mary His mother, "Behold, this Child is appointed for the fall and rise of many in Israel, and for a sign to be opposed—and a sword will pierce even your own soul—to the end that thoughts from many hearts may be revealed."
>
> —Luke 2:34–35

Questions for Reflection

1. Am I having trouble identifying the obstacles to my happiness? If so, what do I think is preventing me from doing this? What can I do to change that?
2. Does it seem like some obstacles to my happiness might be insurmountable? If so, why? Is there anything I can do to change this? If so, what?
3. Aside from the suggestions in this chapter, are there any other things I can do to make my Life Plan something productive?

Appendix 1

Catholic Resources to Answer Your Questions about the Faith

Catholic Radio Resources

Of all the wonderful Catholic radio programs available, the ones listed below are my favorites. These are all live call-in shows with hosts and guests to answer your questions, and all shows air Monday through Friday each week. You can also find most of these as podcasts at iTunes. But the best thing about these shows and their hosts is their goal is to help you clear up any confusion or misunderstandings and help you become more devoted, more in love with your faith.

Ave Maria Radio:

- *The Catholic Connection* with host Teresa Tomeo*
- *The Catholic Business Hour*
- *Fire on the Earth* with host Peter Herbeck*
- *Christ Is the Answer* with host Fr. John Riccardo*

EWTN Radio:

- *Catholic Answers Live* with host Patrick Coffin*
- *EWTN Open Line**
- *Women of Grace* with host Johnnette Benkovic*

Immaculate Heart Radio:

- *Right Here, Right Now* with host Patrick Madrid*

Relevant Radio:

- *On Call* with host Wendy Wiese*
- *Fr. Simon Says*
- *Go Ask Your Father*
- *The Drew Mariani Show**

* *Also available on iTunes*

Online Resources

There are many good websites out there that offer blogs, videos, podcasts, and other content to help you grow in your faith, but they are too many to list. The websites below are my personal favorite "go-to" sites for accurate information and answers:

- DynamicCatholic.com
- AmericanPapist.com
- Catholic Answers (catholic.com)
- CatholicsComeHome.org
- CatholicDadsOnline.org
- CatholicOnline.com
- CreativeMinorityReport.com

- CatholicTherapists.com
- EnvoyInstitute.net
- EWTN Apologetics Library (ewtn.com/library)
- FirstThings.com (subscription)
- Fr. Zuhlsdorf (wdtprs.com/blog)
- National Catholic Register (ncregister.com)
- NewAdvent.org (searchable Catholic encyclopedia)
- PatrickMadrid.com
- St. Charles Borromeo, *Catechism of the Catholic Church* (searchable, scborromeo.org/ccc.htm)
- USCCB.org
- SCBorromeo.org
- Vatican.va
- WomenOfGrace.com
- WordOnFire.org

Appendix 2

Good Reads

Bedard, Vicki Wells, and William E. Rabior. *Prayers for Catholics Experiencing Divorce*. Liguori, MO: Liguori Publications, 2004.

Bennett, Art, and Laraine Bennett. *The Temperament God Gave You: The Classic Key to Knowing Yourself, Getting Along with Others, and Growing Closer to the Lord*. Manchester, NH: Sophia Institute Press, 2005.

Campbell, Ross. *How to Really Love Your Angry Child*. Colorado Springs: Cook Communications, 2004.

Casella-Kapusinski, Lynn. *When Parents Divorce or Separate: I Can Get Through This (Catholic Guide for Kids)*. Boston: Pauline Kids, 2013.

Catholic Book Publishing Corp. *Healing Prayers for Every Day*. Totowa, NJ: Catholic Book Publishing Corp., 2006.

Chapman, Gary D. *The Five Love Languages: The Secret to Love that Lasts*. Chicago: Northfield Publishing, 2010.

Donohue, William. *Why Catholicism Matters: How Catholic Virtues Can Reshape Society in the Twenty-First Century*. New York: Image, 2012.

Hahn, Scott. *Lord, Have Mercy: The Healing Power of Confession*. London: Darton, Longman & Todd, 2003.

Hahn, Scott, and Leon J. Suprenant. *Catholic for a Reason: Scripture and the Mystery of the Family of God*. Steubenville, OH: Emmaus Road Publishing, 1998.

Hampsch, John H. *The Healing Power of the Eucharist*. Cincinnati: St. Anthony Messenger Press, 1999.

John Paul II. *Man and Woman He Created Them: A Theology of the Body*. Translated by Michael Waldstein. Boston: Pauline Books & Media, 2006.

Johnson, Kevin Orlin. *Why Do Catholics Do That? A Guide to the Teachings and Practices of the Catholic Church*. New York: Ballantine Books, 1995.

Kaczor, Christopher. *The Seven Big Myths about the Catholic Church: Distinguishing Fact from Fiction about Catholicism*. San Francisco: Ignatius Press, 2012.

Keating, Karl. *What Catholics Really Believe: 52 Answers to Common Misconceptions about the Catholic Faith*. San Francisco: Ignatius Press, 1995.

Kelly, Elizabeth M. *May Crowning, Mass, and Merton and Other Reasons I Love Being Catholic*. Chicago: Loyola Press, 2006.

Kelly, Matthew. *Rediscover Catholicism*. Boston: Beacon Publishing, 2011.

Kendall, Jackie, and Debby Jones. *Lady in Waiting: Becoming God's Best While Waiting for Mr. Right*. Shippensburg, PA: Destiny Image Publishers, Inc., 2012.

Kresta, Al. *Dangers to the Faith: Recognizing Catholicism's 21st Century Opponents*. Huntington, IN: Our Sunday Visitor, 2013.

Leach, Michael. *Why Stay Catholic? Unexpected Answers to a Life-Changing Question*. Chicago: Loyola Press, 2011.

Lewis, C. S. *Mere Christianity*. C. S. Lewis Signature Classics. San Francisco: Harper San Francisco, 2009.

Lindsay, Jacquelyn. *Catholic Family Prayer Book*. Huntington, IN: Our Sunday Visitor, 2001.

Littauer, Florence, and Rose Sweet. *Personality Plus at Work: How to Work Successfully with Anyone*. Grand Rapids, MI: Revell, 2011.

Madrid, Patrick, ed. *Surprised by Truth: 11 Converts Give the Biblical and Historical Reasons for Becoming Catholic*. Irving, TX: Basilica Press, 1994. (All books by Patrick Madrid are worth checking out.)

Morris, Jonathan. *The Way of Serenity: Finding Peace and Happiness in the Serenity Prayer*. New York: HarperOne, 2014. (All books by Jonathan Morris are worth checking out.)

Pacwa, Mitch. *How to Listen When God Is Speaking: A Guide for Modern-Day Catholics*. Frederick, MD: The Word Among Us Press, 2011.

Peterson, Tom. *Catholics Come Home: God's Extraordinary Plan for Your Life!* New York: Image, 2013.

Popcak, Gregory K. *The Exceptional Seven Percent: The Nine Secrets of the World's Happiest Couples*. New York: Citadel Press Books, 2000.

Ripley, Canon Francis. *This Is the Faith: A Complete Explanation of the Catholic Faith*. Charlotte, NC: TAN Books, 2002.

Rohr, Richard, and Joseph Martos. *Why Be Catholic? Understanding Our Experience and Tradition*. Cincinnati: St. Anthony Messenger Press, 2011.

Schreck, Alan. *Catholic and Christian: An Explanation of Commonly Misunderstood Catholic Beliefs*. Cincinnati: Servant Books, 2004.

Stimpson, Emily. *These Beautiful Bones: An Everyday Theology of the Body*. Steubenville, OH: Emmaus Road Publishing, 2013.

Vere, Pete, and Jacqui Rapp. *Annulment: 100 Questions and Answers for Catholics*. Cincinnati: Servant Books, 2009.

West, Christopher. *Theology of the Body for Beginners: A Basic Introduction to Pope John Paul II's Sexual Revolution*. West Chester, PA: Ascension Press, 2009.

Wojtyla, Karol. *Love and Responsibility*. Translated by H. T. Willetts. San Francisco: Ignatius Press, 1993.

Notes

1. Judith S. Wallerstein, Julia M. Lewis, and Sandra Blakeslee, *The Unexpected Legacy of Divorce: A 25 Year Landmark Study* (New York: Hyperion, 2000), 98.

2. Roberto de la Vega, *Eucharist through the Centuries* (London: Circle Press, 1998), 138.

3. Ibid, 140.

4. C. S. Lewis, *The Four Loves* (New York: Harcourt, 1960), 53.

5. John Paul II, *Man and Woman He Created Them: A Theology of the Body*, trans. Michael Waldstein (Boston: Pauline Books & Media, 2006), 167.

6. Gregory K. Popcak, *The Exceptional Seven Percent: The Nine Secrets of the World's Happiest Couples* (New York: Citadel, 2002), 51.

7. Francis, "Address to Italian and Albanian Students, June 5, 2013," *Vatican Radio*, accessed November 18, 2014, http://en.radiovaticana.va/storico/2013/06/07/pope_tells_students_learn_to_be_magnanimous/en1-699327.

8. Ibid.

9. Mary Reed Newland, *The Saints and Our Children: The Lives of the Saints and Catholic Lessons to be Learned* (New York: TAN Books, 1958).

Lisa Duffy is a Catholic author, speaker, and blogger for the CatholicMatch Institute. A Southern California native, she overcame a painful divorce and annulment, remarried in the Church, and turned to helping other divorced Catholics find hope and healing. She has more than twenty years of experience ministering to those who have been wounded by divorce.

Duffy wrote and directed the popular divorce support program, Journey of Hope, which later became the book *Divorced. Catholic. Now What?* She also directed and produced the powerful *Voices of Hope* DVD. Duffy has contributed to several books and appeared on Relevant Radio, Ave Maria Radio, EWTN TV and radio, Salt and Light TV, and various podcasts. She regularly speaks at conferences for divorced and single Catholics.

Duffy lives in Charleston, South Carolina, with her husband, James, and their three children.